BY ALLEN TATE

COLLECTED POEMS, 1919–1976

ALLEN TATE

COLLECTED POEMS
1919-1976

FARRAR STRAUS GIROUX NEW YORK

Farrar, Straus and Giroux
19 Union Square West, New York 10003

Copyright © 1952, 1953, 1970, 1977 by Allen Tate
Copyright © 1931, 1932, 1937, 1948 by Charles Scribner's Sons
Copyright renewed © 1959, 1960, 1965 by Allen Tate
Introduction copyright © 2001, 2007 by Christopher Benfey
All rights reserved
Distributed in Canada by Douglas & McIntyre Ltd.
Printed in the United States of America
Originally published in 1977 by Farrar, Straus and Giroux
This paperback edition, 2007

The introduction by Christopher Benfey originally appeared, in substantially different form, in the June 4, 2001, issue of *The New Republic*.

Library of Congress Control Number: 2007929096
ISBN-13: 978-0-374-53095-2
ISBN-10: 0-374-53095-5

Designed by Karen Watt

www.fsgbooks.com

P1

TO HELEN

Sunt lacrimae rerum et mentem mortalia tangunt.

*Ne avertas faciem tuam a puero tuo quoniam
tribulor velociter exaudi me.*

CONTENTS

PREFACE

The earliest poem in this volume, "Red Stains," was written in 1919 and the latest, "Farewell Rehearsed," in 1976. The arrangement of the poems, for the most part (except for the "Early Poems" placed at the end, following the translations), is in the order of their first publication. The date following each poem is that of its first appearance in print. This order has been altered in a few cases, however, to place together poems which because of subject matter or presentation should be read in sequence. A few of the poems—"Ode to the Confederate Dead," for example—are followed by two dates, the first being the date of first publication and the second that of the revised, final version included in this volume.

I wish to express my appreciation to two friends, without whose help this book would have been impossible—Monroe K. Spears and Thomas Daniel Young. They assisted me in many ways in preparing this volume, especially in tracking down many heretofore uncollected poems, some of which were never printed. These turned up, through the kindness of Mr. Young, in a typescript of about twenty poems, bound in leather and presented to M.E.H. in June 1922. I had completely forgotten it. It is owned by Edgar H. Duncan, who let me have all of the poems I wanted for this book.

ALLEN TATE

Nashville
January 1977

INTRODUCTION

by Christopher Benfey

In 1949, the year he turned fifty, Allen Tate published an essay called "Our Cousin, Mr. Poe." Tate confessed that as a boy he had stared for hours at "the well-known, desperate, and asymmetrical photograph" of Edgar Allan Poe, whom he hoped he would resemble someday. That wish, as portraits of Tate attest, was granted. But Tate's main point in the essay was not to claim some literal kinship. He argued instead that Poe, the perennial butt of jests and putdowns, deserved a place at the table. "For Americans, perhaps for most modern men, he is with us like a dejected cousin: we may 'place' him but we may not exclude him from our board."*

This is, roughly, our present relationship to Tate himself. Tate is always "placed" as a reactionary Southern critic and poet who played first fiddle (he actually did play the fiddle) in a band of poet-critics called the Fugitives during the twenties, the Agrarians during the thirties, and, augmented with fellow travelers from England and California, the New Critics thereafter. These are the straw men of current literary criticism, the dejected cousins drinking bourbon in the corner, placed but no longer read.

While there is some truth to the gibes directed at the Fugitive–Agrarian–New Critic contingent, they were far more complex and interesting than they are now given credit for. Tate's achievement is both representative of their work at its best and ripe, like a distant cousin, for rediscovery. His distinctive poems; his impressive historical novel, *The Fathers*; his remarkable literary criticism, including some of the best essays ever written on Emily Dickinson and Poe— these won't go away.

*Allen Tate, "Our Cousin, Mr. Poe," in *Essays of Four Decades* (Wilmington, Del.: ISI Books, 1999), 387–88.

Tate was born in the nineteenth century, but barely, in a small town in Kentucky. His father, John Orley Tate, failed at running a lumber firm, the first of many failures as he drifted around the Midwest in search of work, his growing family in tow. According to Tate's biographer, Thomas A. Underwood, Orley was a "powerfully fisted man" prone to "violence, philandering, and drinking."* His son believed that Orley had once killed a black waiter with a chair for spilling soup on him. Tate's mother, by contrast, was petite and prim; her father had owned eighty-one slaves and two hundred thousand acres of timber. Tate's mother and father seemed to their bemused son to embody, respectively, an idealized Old South and the grim realities of the New.

Tate was a sickly child, which suited his smothering mother. Young Allen took violin lessons in Cincinnati, receiving enough encouragement to consider a professional career. At Vanderbilt, he took up the equally sissy practice of writing verse, but balanced it with the manly habits of hard drinking and sex. It was at Vanderbilt, where he enrolled in 1918, that Tate made the friendships of a lifetime, with his mentor, John Crowe Ransom, recently returned from service in World War I, and with his fellow students Robert Penn Warren and Donald Davidson.

While still an undergraduate, Tate became a regular contributor and editor for *The Fugitive*, the literary magazine that he and his friends founded at Vanderbilt. What these men shared was a fierce sense of region and an equally strong conviction that the sentimental and obscurantist ways in which that region had been evoked—the "moon and magnolia" mode—were bankrupt and self-defeating. T. S. Eliot was their hero among the moderns; they were particularly drawn to Eliot's satiric quatrains in such poems as "Sweeney Among the Nightingales" and "Whispers of Immortality."

By 1925, Tate was capable of a sophisticated pastiche like "Mr. Pope," one of his finest early poems:

When Alexander Pope strolled in the city
Strict was the glint of pearl and gold sedans.

*Thomas A. Underwood, *Allen Tate: Orphan of the South* (Princeton: Princeton University Press, 2000), 7.

Ladies leaned out more out of fear than pity
For Pope's tight back was rather a goat's than man's.

Here was an eighteenth-century urbanity, built around wit and opposition (pearl versus gold, fear versus pity, goat versus man), made available to a gentlemanly South.

Tate's early poems attracted more attention in the hated North than in the South. In 1924 he went to New York for the first time and was, he told Davidson, "greatly thrilled at the mere *physique* of this great city!" He was particularly impressed by the subway: "the sheer wonder of it is almost atonement for its significance as a phase of the Triumph of the Machine."* Tate's host in New York was Hart Crane, with whom he had been corresponding for a couple of years. Crane's attempts to find poetic phrasing adequate to describe the modern city influenced Tate's early sonnet "The Subway": "Dark accurate plunger down the successive knell / Of arch on arch, where ogives burst a red Reverberance of hail upon the dead / Thunder..."

Back in the quieter South, Tate moved in with "Red" Warren in Guthrie, Kentucky, where he met Carolyn Gordon, a Chattanooga journalist and aspiring novelist. That fall Tate returned to New York and wrote soft-core pornography for the Climax Publishing Company. Carolyn joined him, and the novelist Ford Madox Ford hired her as his typist. "We were young, we were poor, and we were ambitious," Tate remarked of this circle of friends. "That is, we thought that the older generation was pretty bad, and we were later going to replace them."†

For Tate, Eliot's "The Waste Land" showed a path forward by using symbols to express a certain attitude toward modern rootlessness. Tate's "Ode to the Confederate Dead," published first in 1927, then with revisions ten years later, is, according to Tate's partly tongue-in-cheek essay on the poem, "Narcissus as Narcissus," about the chasm between modern solipsism (a contemporary visitor to a Confederate graveyard) and past heroism (the dead Confederate soldiers).

*Underwood, *Allen Tate*, 99.
†Ibid., 108.

Row after row with strict impunity
The headstones yield their names to the element,
The wind whirrs without recollection;
In the riven troughs the splayed leaves
Pile up, of nature the casual sacrament
To the seasonal eternity of death; . . .

The poem includes lines that are almost comically indebted to Eliot: "Ambitious November with the humors of the year, . . . Night is the beginning and the end / And in between the ends of distraction . . . The gray lean spiders come, they come and go;" (talking, presumably, of Michelangelo). Edmund Wilson, at the time an editor at *Vanity Fair*, returned a batch of Tate's early poems with a note: "I look forward to something extraordinary from you. But do try to get out of the artistic clutches of T. S. Eliot."*

Wilson was wrong about these poems, however. They *were* extraordinary, taking the language of Eliot and directing it toward Southern landscapes and dilemmas. Just what those dilemmas were became clearer to Tate during the decade after the Crash of 1929. The Agrarians—as they now called themselves—were not alone in believing that the United States during the twenties had bet too much on industrialization. What Tate, Warren, and others in the Agrarian group wanted to offer was a whole vision of the good life, based on family farms and the dignity of manual labor. Ritual, too, was on their agenda, and many of the most beautiful poems that arose from the Agrarian moment, like Tate's "Death of Little Boys," have to do with such community-binding rituals as funerals and weddings.

The Southern literary renaissance, Tate decided, had arisen at a "crossing of the ways, not unlike, on an infinitesimal scale, the outburst of poetic genius at the end of the sixteenth century when commercial England had already begun to crush feudal England."† Some such crossing is audible in Tate's own poetry, for Tate as poet has two poetic voices. One is wry and tender, in umbilical touch with childhood—and by extension the "feudal" South. The other is orotund and sublime, a key held up to the sky in hopes of thunder

---

*Underwood, *Allen Tate*, 76.
†Ibid., 217.

and lightning. The opening of "Mr. Pope" is in the former mode; the "Ode" and the impressive "Aeneas in Washington" are in the latter. In Tate's best poems the two voices are in equilibrium, nowhere more poignantly than in "The Swimmers."

> Kentucky water, clear springs: a boy fleeing
> > To water under the dry Kentucky sun,
> > His four little friends in tandem with him, seeing
>
> Long shadows of grapevine wriggle and run
> > Over the green swirl; mullein under the ear
> > Soft as Nausicaä's palm; sullen fun
>
> Savage as childhood's thin harmonious tear:
> > O fountain, bosom source undying-dead
> > Replenish me the spring of love and fear
>
> And give me back the eye that looked and fled
> > When a thrush idling in the tulip tree
> > Unwound the cold dream of the copperhead.

Successful poems in terza rima, the braided rhyme scheme of Dante and of Shelley's "Triumph of Life," are rare in English. Tate's dream vision follows many of the conventions of the genre: the apostrophe to the muse; the sonorous, conjuring language, richest in the sequence of "mullein ... palm ... sullen"; the surveying of border regions of dream and waking, of life and death in the source "undying-dead."

Into this sublime landscape Tate introduces the "shrill companions of that odyssey":

> Bill Eaton, Charlie Watson, 'Nigger' Layne
> > The doctor's son, Harry Duèsler who played
> > The flute; and Tate, with water on the brain.

Seemingly random, matter-of-fact details—the flute player and the hydrocephalic head—undergo a mythical charge in this dreamscape of water music:

Dog-days: the dusty leaves where rain delayed
    Hung low on poison-oak and scuppernong,
    And we were following the active shade

Of water, that bells and bickers all night long.
    'No more'n a mile,' Layne said. All five stood still.
    Listening, I heard what seemed at first a song;

The song turns out to be the hoof-beats of a posse coming down the hill. After a beautifully modulated Homeric simile—"Then, as sleepwalkers shift from a hard place / In bed, and rising to keep a formal pledge / Descend a ladder into empty space, / / We scuttled down the bank below a ledge . . ."—the boys awake to the stark geometry of a lynching. A stranger on horseback and the sheriff drag the body back to town.

My breath crackled the dead air like a shotgun
    As, sheriff and the stranger disappearing,
    The faceless head lay still. I could not run

Or walk, but stood. Alone in the public clearing
    This private thing was owned by all the town,
    Though never claimed by us within my hearing.

Underwood adduces the poem as evidence for Tate's adoption during the 1950s of more progressive views on race.

What "The Swimmers" has to say about Southern guilt may ultimately be less interesting, however, than its exploration of shame and childhood secrets (another haunts the second of the "Sonnets at Christmas"), and how a sense of community is sometimes built, like an oyster with a painful grain of sand, around such secrets. Its power derives from the life of its language, from Tate's sure grip on oneiric evocation, narrative drive, and telling detail. It was Tate's unerring skill in knowing that "scuppernong" and "Harry Duèsler who played the flute" belonged there that makes this poem a key portent of what came to be known, a decade later, as "confessional poetry."

Some of Tate's most appealing poems are in an intimate, almost confiding mode, like "Winter Mask" or the short lyric to Robert Penn Warren called "Brief Message":

This, Warren, is our trouble now:
Not even fools could disavow
Three centuries of piety
Grown bare as a cottonwood tree
(A timber seldom drawn and sawn
And chiefly used to hang men on),
So face with calm that heritage
And earn contempt before the age.

There is more than a hint in that pulsating, plain style of Raleigh and Yeats, but the cottonwood tree—the wayward rhythm of the line in which it is mentioned, and the specialized parenthetical knowledge about its uses—is all Tate's. A young man looks lucidly at the South during the Depression: no religion, no money, a burden of guilt, a bareness of culture, and hostility all around. Under the circumstances, Tate and his friends, those dejected cousins, did okay.

CHRISTOPHER BENFEY is Mellon Professor of English at Mount Holyoke College and the author of a collection of essays titled *American Audacity: Essays North and South*.

PART ONE

Death of Little Boys

When little boys grown patient at last, weary,
Surrender their eyes immeasurably to the night,
The event will rage terrific as the sea;
Their bodies fill a crumbling room with light.

Then you will touch at the bedside, torn in two,
Gold curls now deftly intricate with gray
As the windowpane extends a fear to you
From one peeled aster drenched with the wind all day.

And over his chest the covers in the ultimate dream
Will mount to the teeth, ascend the eyes, press back
The locks—while round his sturdy belly gleam
Suspended breaths, white spars above the wreck:

Till all the guests, come in to look, turn down
Their palms, and delirium assails the cliff
Of Norway where you ponder, and your little town
Reels like a sailor drunk in a rotten skiff.

The bleak sunshine shrieks its chipped music then
Out to the milkweed amid the fields of wheat.
There is a calm for you where men and women
Unroll the chill precision of moving feet.

1925

Homily

If thine eye offend thee, pluck it out.

If your tired unspeaking head
Rivet the dark with linear sight,
Crazed by a warlock with his curse
Dreamed up in some loquacious bed,
And if the stage-dark head rehearse
The fifth act of the closing night,

Why, cut it off, piece after piece,
And throw the tough cortex away,
And when you've marvelled on the wars
That wove their interior smoke its way,
Tear out the close vermiculate crease
Where death crawled angrily at bay.

1925

Madness

The wardrobe towers above the table lamp,
The harpsichord stands sentinel between;
The clock's tin argument whines out its damp
Terror, like an eyelid winking through a screen.

Young bats around the hills like sands are whirring
Past clouds of roosting vultures sick with flight,
Till the rag carpet on the hardwood stirring
Wrinkles to winds which are a swift delight.

Impanelled walls, raging with gloom, abound
In commonplaces to moralize the eye—
Which are white cats whose slick metallic sound
Cuts to the heart with a half-completed lie.

And ladies with their nails prepared for tea
And sunken barques that coast the shores of hell
And old men vacant of propriety
Have faintly rung a next-door neighbor's bell.

On the iron cot the coverlets are neat
With the bold care of an ecstatic trull
Who rearranges with impartial feet
The silence in the caverns of a skull.

1925

Mr. Pope

When Alexander Pope strolled in the city
Strict was the glint of pearl and gold sedans.
Ladies leaned out more out of fear than pity
For Pope's tight back was rather a goat's than man's.

Often one thinks the urn should have more bones
Than skeletons provide for speedy dust,
The urn gets hollow, cobwebs brittle as stones
Weave to the funeral shell a frivolous rust.

And he who dribbled couplets like a snake
Coiled to a lithe precision in the sun
Is missing. The jar is empty; you may break
It only to find that Mr. Pope is gone.

What requisitions of a verity
Prompted the wit and rage between his teeth
One cannot say. Around a crooked tree
A moral climbs whose name should be a wreath.

1925

To a Romantic

To Robert Penn Warren

You hold your eager head
Too high in the air, you walk
As if the sleepy dead
Had never fallen to drowse
From the sublimest talk
Of many a vehement house.
Your head so turned turns eyes
Into the vagrant West;
Fixing an iron mood
In an Ozymandias' breast
And because your clamorous blood
Beats an impermanent rest
You think the dead arise
Westward and fabulous:
The dead are those whose lies
Were doors to a narrow house.

1924

To a Romantic Novelist

Now that you've written it
In novels and a few verses,
Will the pimps and harlots say
That Destiny's a wit?
Will the coarse kitchen-wench
Think she's Desiree
For the policeman's visit?
She's hardly such a coward.
For when it comes to that
You seem to be looking toward
A meagre public fate
—Swelling damnedly fat—
With a rhetorical hate.
I think Petronius
Would not have let you in
(With Mencken and Hergesheimer)
In that smugly cankerous
Incertitude of taste.
Scan the popular stench
With wit: the actor rehearses
To the flattered arbiter.
And what's the bother about sin?
It doesn't matter so
Whether a woman's unchaste.
Talk to Trimalchio.

1925

Ditty

The moon will run all consciences to cover,
Night is now the easy peer of day;
Little boys no longer sight the plover
Streaked in the sky, and cattle go
Warily out in search of misty hay.
Look at the blackbird, the pretty eager swallow,
The buzzard, and all the birds that sail
With the smooth essential flow
Of time through men, who fail.

For now the moon with friendless light carouses
On hill and housetop, street and marketplace,
Men will plunge, mile after mile of men,
To crush this lucent madness of the face,
Go home and put their heads upon the pillow,
Turn with whatever shift the darkness cleaves,
Tuck in their eyes, and cover
The flying dark with sleep like falling leaves.

1926

Idyl

In a valley late bees with whining gold
Thread summer to the loose ends of sleep;
A harvester pauses, surprised, in dreams of sheep,
Across his back the ravellings of the sun.

No risk of incandescence begs his eyes
To the stubble horizon, nor ceremony
Of season slipping absently to fall;
Only the endless water in the run.

If always the torture of stillness suddenly
Argued so brisk and vain an agony,
One hid in winter could look back and say:

"Summer, you are the eucharist of death;
Partake of you and never again
Will midnight foot it steeply into dawn,
Dawn veer into day,
Nor the praised schism be of year split off year.
All time would be some tatters
On a figure, and the arrested sun—
Which are one."

1926

Retroduction to American History

Cats walk the floor at midnight; that enemy of fog,
The moon, wraps the bedpost in receding stillness; sleep
Collects all weary nothings and lugs away the towers,
The pinnacles of dust that feed the subway.

What stiff unhappy silence waits on sleep
Struts like an officer; tongues next-door bewitch
Themselves with divination; I like a melancholy oaf
Beg the nightly pillow with impossible loves.
And abnegation folds hands, crossed like the knees
Of the complacent tailor, stitches cloaks of mercy
To the backs of obsessions.

                                 Winter like spring no less
Tolerates the air; the wild pheasant meets innocently
The gun; night flouts illumination with meagre impudence.
In such serenity of equal fates, why has Narcissus
Urged the brook with questions? Merged with the element
Speculation suffuses the meadow with drops to tickle
The cow's gullet; grasshoppers drink the rain.
Antiquity breached mortality with myths.
Narcissus is vocabulary. Hermes decorates
A cornice on the Third National Bank. Vocabulary
Becomes confusion, decoration a blight; the Parthenon
In Tennessee stucco, art for the sake of death. Now
(The bedpost receding in stillness) you brush your teeth
'Hitting on all thirty-two'; scholarship pares
The nails of Catullus, sniffs his sheets, restores
His 'passionate underwear'; morality disciplines the other
Person; every son-of-a-bitch is Christ, at least Rousseau;
Prospero serves humanity in steam-heated universities, three

Thousand dollars a year. Simplicity, Flamineo, is obscene;
Sunlight topples indignant from the hill.
In every railroad station everywhere every lover
Waits for his train. He cannot hear. The smoke
Thickens. Ticket in hand, he pumps his body
Toward lower six, for one more terse ineffable trip,
His very eyeballs fixed in disarticulation. The berth
Is clean; no elephants, vultures, mice or spiders
Distract him from nonentity: his metaphors are dead.

More sanitation is enough, enough remains: dreams
Do not end—lucidities beyond the stint of thought.
For intellect is a mansion where waste is without drain;
A corpse is your bedfellow, your great-grandfather dines
With you this evening on a cavalry horse. Intellect
Connives with heredity, creates fate as Euclid geometry
By definition:

> The sunlit bones in your house
> Are immortal in the titmouse,
> They trip the feet of grandma
> Like an afterthought each day.
> These unseen sunlit bones,
> They may be in the cat
> That startles them in grandma
> But look at this or that
> They meet you every way.

For Pelops' and Tantalus' successions were at once
    simpler,
If perplexed, and less subtle than you think. Heredity
Proposes love, love exacts language, and we lack
Language. When shall we speak again? When shall
The sparrow dusting the gutter sing? When shall
This drift with silence meet the sun? When shall I wake?

1926

Causerie

... *party on the stage of the Earl Carroll Theatre on Feb. 23. At this party Joyce Hawley, a chorus-girl, bathed in the nude in a bathtub filled with alleged wine.*—The New York Times

What are the springs of sleep? What is the motion
Of dust in the lane that has an end in falling?
Heroes, heroes, you auguries of passion,
Where are the heroes with sloops and telescopes
Who got out of bed at four to vex the dawn?
Men for their last quietus scanned the earth,
Alert on the utmost foothill of the mountains;
They were the men who climbed the topmost screen
Of the world, if sleep but lay beyond it,
Sworn to the portage of our confirmed sensations,
Seeking our image in the farthest hills.
Now bearing a useless testimony of strife
Gathered in a rumor of light, we know our end
A packet of worm-seed, a garden of spent tissues.
I've done no rape, arson, incest, no murder,
Yet cannot sleep. The petty crimes of silence
(Wary pander to whom the truth's chief whore)
I have omitted; no fool can say my tongue
Reversed its fetish and made a cult of conscience.
This innermost disturbance is a babble,
It is a sign moved to my face as well
Where every tide of heart surges to speech
Until in that loquacity of visage
One speaks a countenance fitter for death than hell.
Always your features lean to one direction
And by that charted distance know your doom.
For death is 'morality touched with emotion,'
The syllable and full measure of affirmation;
Give life the innocent crutch of quiet fools.

Where is your house, in which room stands your bed?
What window discovers these insupportable dreams?
In a lean house spawned on baked limestone
Blood history is the murmur of grasshoppers
Eastward of the dawn. Have you a daughter,
Daughters are the seed of occupations,
Of asperities, such as wills, deeds, mortgages,
Duels, estates, statesmen, pioneers, embezzlers,
'Eminent Virginians,' reminiscences, bastards,
The bar-sinister hushed, effaced by the porcelain tub.
A daughter is the fruit of occupations;
Let her not read history lest knowledge
Of her fathers instruct her to be a petty bawd.
Vittoria was herself, the contemporary strumpet
A plain bitch.

       For miracles are faint
And resurrection is our weakest clause of religion,
I have known men in my youth who foundered on
This point of doctrine: John Ransom, boasting hardy
Entelechies yet botched in the head, lacking grace;
Warren thirsty in Kentucky, his hair in the rain, asleep;
None so unbaptized as Edmund Wilson the unwearied,
That sly parody of the devil. They lacked doctrine;
They waited. I, who watched out the first crisis
With them, wait:

       For the incredible image. Now
I am told that Purusha sits no more in our eyes.
Year after year the blood of Christ will sleep
In the holy tree, the branches sagged without bloom
Till the plant overflowing the stale vegetation
In May the creek swells with the anemone,
The Lord God wastes his substance towards the ocean.
In Christ we have lived, on the flood of Christ borne up,

Who now is a precipitate flood of silence,
We a drenched wreck off an imponderable shore:
A jagged cloud is our memory of shore
Whereon we figure hills below ultimate ranges.
You cannot plot the tendency of man,
Whither it leads is not mysterious
In the various grave; but whence the impulse
To lust for the apple of apples on Christ's tree,
To desire in the eye, to penetrate your sleep,
Perhaps to catch in unexpected leaves
The light incentive of your absolute suspicion?
Over the mountains, the last barrier, you'd spill
These relics of your sires in a pool of sleep,
The sun being drained.

                         We have learned to require
In the infirm concessions of memory
The privilege never to hear too much.
What is this conversation, now secular,
A speech not mine yet speaking for me in
The heaving jelly of my tribal air?
It rises in the throat, it climbs the tongue,
It perches there for secret tutelage
And gets it, of inscrutable instruction—
Which is a puzzle like crepuscular light
That has no visible source but fills the trees
With equal foliage, as if the upper leaf
No less than the under were only imminent shade.
Manhood like a lawyer with his formulas
Sesamés his youth for innocent acquittal.

The essential wreckage of your age is different,
The accident the same; the Annabella
Of proper incest, no longer incestuous:
In an age of abstract experience, fornication
Is self-expression, adjunct to Christian euphoria,
And whores become delinquents; delinquents, patients;
Patients, wards of society. Whores, by that rule,
Are precious.

              Was it for this that Lucius
Became the ass of Thessaly? For this did Kyd
Unlock the lion of passion on the stage?
To litter a race of politic pimps? To glut
The Capitol with the progeny of thieves—
Where now the antique courtesy of your myths
Goes in to sleep under a still shadow?

1927

Idiot

The idiot greens the meadow with his eyes,
The meadow creeps implacable and still;
A dog barks, the hammock swings, he lies.
One two three the cows bulge on the hill.

Motion that is not time erects snowdrifts
While sister's hand sieves waterfalls of lace.
With a palm fan closer than death he lifts
The Ozarks and tilted seas across his face.

In the long sunset where impatient sound
Strips niggers to a multiple of backs
Flies yield their heat, magnolias drench the ground
With Appomattox! The shadows lie in stacks.

The julep glass weaves echoes in Jim's kinks
While ashy Jim puts murmurs in the day;
Now in the idiot's heart a chamber stinks
Of dead asters, as the potter's field of May.

All evening the marsh is a slick pool
Where dream wild hares, witch hazel, pretty girls.
'Up from the important picnic of a fool
Those rotted asters!' Eddy on eddy swirls

The innocent mansion of a panther's heart!
It crumbles, tick-tick time drags it in
Till now his arteries lag and now they start
Reverence with the frigid gusts of sin.

The stillness pelts the eye, assaults the hair;
A beech sticks out a branch to warn the stars,
A lightning-bug jerks angles in the air,
Diving. 'I am the captain of new wars!'

The dusk runs down the lane driven like hail;
Far off a precise whistle is escheat
To the dark; and then the towering weak and pale
Covers his eyes with memory like a sheet.

1927

The Subway

Dark accurate plunger down the successive knell
Of arch on arch, where ogives burst a red
Reverberance of hail upon the dead
Thunder like an exploding crucible!
Harshly articulate, musical steel shell
Of angry worship, hurled religiously
Upon your business of humility
Into the iron forestries of hell:

Till broken in the shift of quieter
Dense altitudes tangential of your steel,
I am become geometries, and glut
Expansions like a blind astronomer
Dazed, while the worldless heavens bulge and reel
In the cold revery of an idiot.

1927

Ode to the Confederate Dead

Row after row with strict impunity
The headstones yield their names to the element,
The wind whirrs without recollection;
In the riven troughs the splayed leaves
Pile up, of nature the casual sacrament
To the seasonal eternity of death;
Then driven by the fierce scrutiny
Of heaven to their election in the vast breath,
They sough the rumour of mortality.

Autumn is desolation in the plot
Of a thousand acres where these memories grow
From the inexhaustible bodies that are not
Dead, but feed the grass row after rich row.
Think of the autumns that have come and gone!—
Ambitious November with the humors of the year,
With a particular zeal for every slab,
Staining the uncomfortable angels that rot
On the slabs, a wing chipped here, an arm there:
The brute curiosity of an angel's stare
Turns you, like them, to stone,
Transforms the heaving air
Till plunged to a heavier world below
You shift your sea-space blindly
Heaving, turning like the blind crab.

Dazed by the wind, only the wind
The leaves flying, plunge

You know who have waited by the wall
The twilight certainty of an animal,
Those midnight restitutions of the blood
You know—the immitigable pines, the smoky frieze
Of the sky, the sudden call: you know the rage,
The cold pool left by the mounting flood,
Of muted Zeno and Parmenides.
You who have waited for the angry resolution
Of those desires that should be yours tomorrow,
You know the unimportant shrift of death
And praise the vision
And praise the arrogant circumstance
Of those who fall
Rank upon rank, hurried beyond decision—
Here by the sagging gate, stopped by the wall.

    Seeing, seeing only the leaves
    Flying, plunge and expire

Turn your eyes to the immoderate past,
Turn to the inscrutable infantry rising
Demons out of the earth—they will not last.
Stonewall, Stonewall, and the sunken fields of hemp,
Shiloh, Antietam, Malvern Hill, Bull Run.
Lost in that orient of the thick-and-fast
You will curse the setting sun.

    Cursing only the leaves crying
    Like an old man in a storm

You hear the shout, the crazy hemlocks point
With troubled fingers to the silence which
Smothers you, a mummy, in time.

                                    The hound bitch
Toothless and dying, in a musty cellar
Hears the wind only.

                            Now that the salt of their blood
Stiffens the saltier oblivion of the sea,
Seals the malignant purity of the flood,
What shall we who count our days and bow
Our heads with a commemorial woe
In the ribboned coats of grim felicity,
What shall we say of the bones, unclean,
Whose verdurous anonymity will grow?
The ragged arms, the ragged heads and eyes
Lost in these acres of the insane green?
The gray lean spiders come, they come and go;
In a tangle of willows without light
The singular screech-owl's tight
Invisible lyric seeds the mind
With the furious murmur of their chivalry.

        We shall say only the leaves
        Flying, plunge and expire

We shall say only the leaves whispering
In the improbable mist of nightfall
That flies on multiple wing;
Night is the beginning and the end
And in between the ends of distraction
Waits mute speculation, the patient curse
That stones the eyes, or like the jaguar leaps
For his own image in a jungle pool, his victim.
What shall we say who have knowledge
Carried to the heart? Shall we take the act
To the grave? Shall we, more hopeful, set up the grave
In the house? The ravenous grave?

                                        Leave now
The shut gate and the decomposing wall:
The gentle serpent, green in the mulberry bush,
Riots with his tongue through the hush—
Sentinel of the grave who counts us all!

1927 / 1937

The Progress of Œnia

His olim, ut fama est, vitiis ad proelia ventum est,
bis Troiana vides funera principiis.—Propertius

I. MADRIGALE

Seed in your heart, warm dust transmuted
Gold, blooms in flakes of radiance
Arched in your face whereon my days,
Brinks of silence, glance.

Dream-emptied by some shifting
Monna Bice, you I resume:
Continually suffer the habitual
Cobra of my slightest gloom!

Release the happy hounds that trace
New smiles from the scampering wood
Of winter laughters—new prints of light
And trace them to your face!

II. IN WINTERTIME

I would not give the winter for a rose.
For remembering gold meadows and the hummer
Sucking them, I think June a time of pillage.
Your mouth is more passionate than any summer.

They say the spring holds many grapes
And green promises of fruit in the summer.
Give me your lips, Œnia, and let winter seas
Lash the cliffs and snows bite the grape.
We shall have passion without the sound of bees.

III. VIGIL

When you are dead and the frosty iron of laughter
Stupendously settles its pride upon your lips,
I will gather up the whispers you came after
When we first met, of immutable dissimulation.

If you are dead when the wind cries again
Over the bleak gables of an expected hour,
I will build a chapel out of the astonished pain
And wait for bells ringing in an empty tower.

IV. DIVAGATION

How many winds forget the sea!
Your dubious intention I forget
And look into the eager waste
Of your eyes careless of yesterday.

What cruel wine, what wayward gust
Tattering sun-hair to shreds of rain,
Swept you an exile to Cyrene
Blown by the swollen winds of pain,

I do not know, for we are dead:
Cluttering our youthful peace
With a various insolence, you laugh
The year, avid of love, to grief!

Our death, that was lonely, you've forgot;
Dawn came to us impatiently
Then went away with an equal fire,
Yet in an instant, in lifted night,

This desolation is alive
With backward motions of bright feet—
Remembering the madness of scaling
A certain dusk to the first small star.

V. EPILOGUE TO ŒNIA

Whatever I have said to praise
Your wrath for me in better days
Than these, when the toughening grass
Fell tenderer for you to pass,
I say again, but differently—
As a still wind in a winter tree.
Pardon me! if turning over
In the reminiscence of a lover
The leaves of a desiccate romance,
I can but wonder if a chance
Invasion of a handsomer look
Than mine began you another book?
I shan't devise the same end
For other books—unless you send
Me word demanding back your hair.

Do you remember how your hair
Contained both ears? It never hid
Them quite, but climbed to a pyramid
More dazzling than superstitious kings
Set in the sand as their playthings;
And tell me, was it wantonness
Fluttering a diaphanous dress
That night at the Club when polite backs
Jazzed to the midnight cordax
And my veins raced to Seboim:
Not wantonness, but you were slim,
My dear, with a gift that I admired
For always being somehow tired!

Whatever else I say, your breast
Contained the witchery of the rest
Of a body vanished into a thought
If touched too late, or lately caught.
So more than your hair or olive eye
I remember your breast—does it still lie
Tactual billows in an upper world
Of superior sculpture, whence you hurled
Volcanic innocence and death
Out of the caverns beneath breath?
Œnia! forgive these sentiments
Of a respectful lover shattered in sense—
Yet sad that the modern bawd, grown dim,
Obscures the hotel cherubim
Whose red neckties had honored this page
In a hotter, less barbaric age;
For now the languid stertorous
Pale verses of Propertius
And the sapphire corpse undressed by Donne
(Prefiguring Rimbaud's etymon)
Have shrunk to an apotheosis
Of cold daylight after the kiss.

And since helmets of steel bone rind
The great heads of the Numerous Mind
No glories of your breast and thighs
Shall these poor verses advertise—
Only the dry debility
Of a spent wind in a winter tree.

1928

Sonnet to Beauty

The wonder of light is your familiar tale,
Pert wench, down to the nineteenth century:
Mr. Rimbaud the Frenchman's apostasy
Asserts the argument that you are stale,
Flat and unprofitable, importunate but pale,
Lithe Corpse! His defect of philosophy
Impugned, but could not strip your entity
Of light. Broken, our twilit visions fail.

Beauty, the doctrine of the incorporate Word
Conceives your fame; how else should you subsist?
The present age, beak southward, flies like a bird—
For often at Church I've seen the stained high glass
Pour out the Virgin and Saints, twist and untwist
The mortal youth of Christ astride an ass.

1928

The Eagle

Say never the strong heart
In the consuming breath
Cries out unto the dark
The skinny death.

Look! whirring on the rind
Of æther a white eagle,
Shot out of the mind,
The windy apple, burning,

Hears no more, past compass
In his topless flight,
The apple wormed, blown up
By shells of light;

So, faggot of the heart
On the cinder day—
The woman and the man!
David and Sybil say

The world has a season
Under the world's might:
Now in deep autumn—
Black apple in the night.

Think not the world spins ever
(Only the world has a year)
Only the gaunt fierce bird
Flies, merciless with fear

Lest air hold him not,
Beats up the scaffold of space
Sick of the world's rot—
God's hideous face.

1929

Historical Epitaphs

I. ON THE FATHER OF LIBERTY

Jefferson had many charms;
Was democratic; still—and yet
What should one do? The family arms
On coach and spoon he wisely set
Against historical alarms:
For quality not being loath,
Nor quantity, nor the fame of both.

II. ON THE GREAT CONCILIATOR: NOW HONORED IN THE OLD DOMINION

'Tis said the Honorable Henry Clay
Was poor-white stock of Hanover,
And left Virginia for the New Day
(Kentucky) where the strong men were:
A ruffled shirt and a gilded coach,
Along with ambition, changed their mind—
At least the Virginians now are kind.
Such was the sting of their reproach.

III. ON THE FOUNDER OF THE INDUSTRIAL SYSTEM IN THE UNITED STATES

In Webster and the town of Slatersville
Samuel Slater, builder of Slater's Mill,
Owned the white hands of men, but not a slave;
Better that Negroes, the well-fed heroic wave
(Its echoes crashing in Atlanta still),
Crashed against Lee at the Foot of Marye's Hill.

IV. ON THE MARTYR OF HARPERS FERRY

John Brown of Ossawattamie
Who died to set Abstraction free
Stole Washington's gold-handled sword
Less for the gold than for the Lord:
It cannot be it would amuse
The General, could he hear the news.

1930

The Cross

There is a place that some men know,
I cannot see the whole of it
Nor how I came there. Long ago
Flame burst out of a secret pit
Crushing the world with such a light
The day-sky fell to moonless black,
The kingly sun to hateful night
For those, once seeing, turning back:
For love so hates mortality
Which is the providence of life
She will not let it blesséd be
But curses it with mortal strife,
Until beside the blinding rood
Within that world-destroying pit
—Like young wolves that have tasted blood—
Of death, men taste no more of it.
So blind, in so severe a place
(All life before in the black grave)
The last alternatives they face
Of life, without the life to save,
Being from all salvation weaned—
A stag charged both at heel and head:
Who would come back is turned a fiend
Instructed by the fiery dead.

1930

Mother and Son

Now all day long the man who is not dead
Hastens the dark with inattentive eyes,
The woman with white hand and erect head
Stares at the covers, leans for the son's replies
At last to her importunate womanhood—
Her hand of death laid on the living bed;
So lives the fierce compositor of blood.

She waits; he lies upon the bed of sin
Where greed, avarice, anger writhed and slept
Till to their silence they were gathered in:
There, fallen with time, his tall and bitter kin
Once fired the passions that were never kept
In the permanent heart, and there his mother lay
To bear him on the impenetrable day.

The falcon mother cannot will her hand
Up to the bed, nor break the manacle
His exile sets upon her harsh command
That he should say the time is beautiful—
Transfigured by her own possessing light:
The sick man craves the impalpable night.

Loosed betwixt eye and lid, the swimming beams
Of memory, blind school of cuttlefish,
Rise to the air, plunge to the cold streams—
Rising and plunging the half-forgotten wish
To tear his heart out in a slow disgrace
And freeze the hue of terror to her face.

Hate, misery, and fear beat off his heart
To the dry fury of the woman's mind;
The son, prone in his autumn, moves apart
A seed blown upon a returning wind.
O child, be vigilant till towards the south
On the flowered wall all the sweet afternoon,
The reaching sun, swift as the cottonmouth,
Strikes at the black crucifix on her breast
Where the cold dusk comes suddenly to rest—
Mortality will speak the victor soon!

The dreary flies, lazy and casual,
Stick to the ceiling, buzz along the wall.
O heart, the spider shuffles from the mould
Weaving, between the pinks and grapes, his pall.
The bright wallpaper, imperishably old,
Uncurls and flutters, it will never fall.

1930

Emblems

Maryland, Virginia, Caroline
Pent images in sleep
Clay valleys rocky hills old fields of pine
Unspeakable and deep

Out of that source of time my farthest blood
Runs strangely to this day
Unkempt the fathers waste in solitude
Under the hills of clay

Far from their woe fled to its thither side
To a river in Tennessee
In an alien house I will stay
Yet find their breath to be
All that my stars betide—
There some time to abide
Took wife and child with me.

II

When it is all over and the blood
Runs out, do not bury this man
By the far river (where never stood
His fathers) flowing to the West,
But take him East where life began.
O my brothers, there is rest
In the depths of an eastward river
That I can understand; only
Do not think the truth we hold
I hold the slighter for this lonely
Reservation of the heart:

Men cannot live forever
But they must die forever
So take this body at sunset
To the great stream whose pulses start
In the blue hills, and let
These ashes drift from the Long Bridge
Where only a late gull breaks
That deep and populous grave.

III

By the great river the forefathers to beguile
Them, being inconceivably young, carved out
Deep hollows of memory on a river isle
Now lost—their murmur the ghost of a shout

In the hollows where the forefathers
Without beards, their faces bright and long,
Lay down at sunset by the cool river
In the tall willows amid birdsong;

And the long sleep by the cool river
They've slept full and long, till now the air
Waits twilit for their echo; the burning shiver
Of August strikes like a hawk the crouching hare.

1931

Last Days of Alice

Alice grown lazy, mammoth but not fat,
Declines upon her lost and twilight age;
Above in the dozing leaves the grinning cat
Quivers forever with his abstract rage:

Whatever light swayed on the perilous gate
Forever sways, nor will the arching grass,
Caught when the world clattered, undulate
In the deep suspension of the looking-glass.

Bright Alice! always pondering to gloze
The spoiled cruelty she had meant to say
Gazes learnedly down her airy nose
At nothing, nothing thinking all the day.

Turned absent-minded by infinity
She cannot move unless her double move,
The All-Alice of the world's entity
Smashed in the anger of her hopeless love,

Love for herself who, as an earthly twain,
Pouted to join her two in a sweet one;
No more the second lips to kiss in vain
The first she broke, plunged through the glass alone—

Alone to the weight of impassivity,
Incest of spirit, theorem of desire,
Without will as chalky cliffs by the sea,
Empty as the bodiless flesh of fire:

All space, that heaven is a dayless night,
A nightless day driven by perfect lust
For vacancy, in which her bored eyesight
Stares at the drowsy cubes of human dust.

—We too back to the world shall never pass
Through the shattered door, a dumb shade-harried crowd
Being all infinite, function depth and mass
Without figure, a mathematical shroud

Hurled at the air—blesséd without sin!
O God of our flesh, return us to Your wrath,
Let us be evil could we enter in
Your grace, and falter on the stony path!

1931

Message from Abroad

To Andrew Lytle

Paris, November 1929

Their faces are bony and sharp but very red, although their ancestors nearly two hundred years have dwelt by the miasmal banks of tidewaters where malarial fever makes men gaunt and dosing with quinine shakes them as with a palsy.—Traveller to America (1799)

I

What years of the other times, what centuries
Broken, divided up and claimed? A few
Here and there to the taste, in vigilance
Ceaseless, but now a little stale, to keep us
Fearless, not worried as the hare scurrying
Without memory . . .

Provence,
The Renascence, the age of Pericles, each
A broad, rich-carpeted stair to pride
With manhood now the cost—they're easy to follow
For the ways taken are all notorious,
Lettered, sculptured, and rhymed;
Those others, incuriously complete, lost,
Not by poetry and statues timed,
Shattered by sunlight and the impartial sleet.
What years . . . What centuries . . .

Now only
The bent eaves and the windows cracked,
The thin grass picked by the wind,
Heaved by the mole; the hollow pine that
Screams in the latest storm—these,
These emblems of twilight have we seen at length,
And the man red-faced and tall seen, leaning

In the day of his strength
Not as a pine, but the stiff form
Against the west pillar,
Hearing the ox-cart in the street—
His shadow gliding, a long nigger
Gliding at his feet.

II

Wanderers to the east, wanderers west:
I followed the cold northern track,
The sleet sprinkled the sea;
The dim foam mounted
The night, the ship mounted
The depths of night—
How absolute the sea!

With dawn came the gull to the crest,
Stared at the spray, fell asleep
Over the picked bones, the white face
Of the leaning man drowned deep;

The red-faced man, ceased wandering,
Never came to the boulevards
Nor covertly spat in the sawdust
Sunk in his collar
Shuffling the cards;

The man with the red face, the stiff back,
I cannot see in the rainfall
Down Saint-Michel by the quays,
At the corner the wind speaking
Destiny, the four ways.

III

I cannot see you
The incorruptibles,
Yours was a secret fate,
The stiff-backed liars, the dupes:
The universal blue
Of heaven rots,
Your anger is out of date—
What did you say mornings?
Evenings, what?
The bent eaves
On the cracked house,
That ghost of a hound. . . .
The man red-faced and tall
Will cast no shadow
From the province of the drowned.

1931

The Oath

It was near evening, the room was cold
Half dark; Uncle Ben's brass bullet-mould
And powder-horn and Major Bogan's face
Above the fire in the half-light plainly said:
There's naught to kill but the animated dead.
Horn nor mould nor major follows the chase.
Being cold I urged Lytle to the fire
In the blank twilight with not much left untold
By two old friends when neither's a great liar.
We sat down evenly in the smoky chill.
There's precious little to say between day and dark,
Perhaps a few words on the implacable will
Of time sailing like a magic barque
Or something as fine for the amenities,
Till dusk seals the window, the fire grows bright,
And the wind saws the hill with a swarm of bees.
Now meditating a little on the firelight
We heard the darkness grapple with the night
And give an old man's valedictory wheeze
From his westward breast between his polar jaws;
Then Lytle asked: Who are the dead?
Who are the living and the dead?
And nothing more was said.
So I, leaving Lytle to that dream,
Decided what it is in time that gnaws
The ageing fury of a mountain stream
When suddenly as an ignorant mind will do
I thought I heard the dark pounding its head
On a rock, crying: *Who are the dead?*
Then Lytle turned with an oath—By God it's true!

The Twelve

There by some wrinkled stones round a leafless tree
With beards askew, their eyes dull and wild
Twelve ragged men, the council of charity
Wandering the face of the earth a fatherless child,
Kneel, at their infidelity aghast,
For where was it, somewhere in Syria
Or Palestine when the streams went red,
The victor of Rome, his arms outspread,
His eyes cold with his inhuman ecstasy,
Cried the last word, the accursed last
Of the forsaken that seared the western heart
With the fire of the wind, the thick and the fast
Whirl of the damned in the heavenly storm:
Now the wind's empty and the twelve living dead
Look round them for that promontory Form
Whose mercy flashed from the sheet lightning's head;
But the twelve lie in the sand by the dry rock
Seeing nothing—the sand, the tree, rocks
Without number—and turn away the face
To the mind's briefer and more desert place.

1931

The Paradigm

For when they meet, the tensile air
Like fine steel strains under the weight
Of messages that both hearts bear—
Pure passion once, now purest hate;

Till the taut air like a cold hand
Clasped to cold hand and bone to bone
Seals them up in their icy land
(A few square feet) where into stone

The two hearts turning quickly pass
Once more their impenetrable world;
So fades out each heart's looking-glass
Whose image is the surface hurled

By all the air; air, glass is not;
So is their fleeting enmity
Like a hard mirror crashed by what
The quality of air must be.

For in the air all lovers meet
After they've hated out their love;
Love's but the echo of retreat
Caught by the sunbeam stretched above

Their frozen exile from the earth
And lost. Each is the other's crime.
This is their equity in birth—
Hate is its ignorant paradigm.

1931

PART TWO

Sonnets of the Blood

I

What is the flesh and blood compounded of
But a few moments in the life of time?
This prowling of the cells, litigious love,
Wears the long claw of flesh-arguing crime.
Consider the first settlers of our bone,
Observe how busily they sued the dust,
Estopped forever by the last dusted stone.
It is a pity that two brothers must
Perceive a canker of perennial flower
To make them brothers in mortality:
Perfect this treason to the murderous hour
If you would win the hard identity
Of brothers—a long race for men to run
Nor quite achieved when the perfection's won.

II

Near to me as perfection in the blood
And more mysterious far, is this, my brother:
A light vaulted into your solitude.
It studied burns lest you its rage should smother.
It is a flame obscure to any eyes,
Most like the fire that warms the deepest grave
(The cold grave is the deepest of our lies)
To which our blood is the indentured slave:
The fire that burns most secretly in you
Does not expend you hidden and alone,
The studious fire consumes not one, but two—
Me also, marrowing the self-same bone.
Our property in fire is death in life
Flawing the rocky fundament with strife.

III

Then, brother, you would never think me vain
Or rude, if I should mention dignity;
Think little of it. Dignity's the stain
Of mortal sin that knows humility.
Let me design the hour when you were born
Since, if that's vain, it's only childlike so:
Like an attempting frost on April corn
Considerate death would hardly let you go.
Reckon the cost—if you would validate
Once more our slavery to circumstance
Not by contempt of a prescriptive fate
But in your bearing towards an hour of chance.
It is a part so humble and so proud
You'll think but little of it in your shroud.

IV

The times have changed. Why do you make a fuss
For privilege when there's no law of form?
Who of our kin was pusillanimous,
A fine bull galloping into a storm?
Why, none; unless you count it arrogance
To cultivate humility in pride,
To look but casually and half-askance
On boots and spurs that went a devil's ride.
There was, remember, a Virginian
Who took himself to be brute nature's law,
Cared little what men thought him, a tall man
Who meditated calmly what he saw
Until he freed his Negroes, lest he be
Too strict with nature and than they less free.

V

These generations that have sealed your heart
Against the neighborly and easy joy
Prefigured you to take the quiet part
Of the secret mind while you were still a boy,
Nay before that for it had all begun—
Even your courage to accept that fate
In Shenandoah and along Bull Run
Sunk in a time inimical to date,
Wherefore you're ridden by time anxious of hours
As a right tackle crouched upon the line
Awaits the snapper-back before he towers
Like granite, risen in the fall sunshine
And towering higher when as the play begins,
His team's thrown back, and loses as he wins.

VI

Our elder brother whom we had not seen
These twenty years until you brought him back
From the cyclonic West, where he had been
Sent by the shaking fury in the track
We know so well, wound in these arteries:
You, other brother, I have become strange
To you, and you must study ways to seize
Mortality, that knows how to derange
Corpuscles for designs that it may choose;
Your blood is altered by the sudden death
Of one who of all persons could not use
Life half so well as death. Let's look beneath
That life. Perhaps hers only is our rest—
To study this, all lifetime may be best.

VII

The fire I praise was once perduring flame—
Till it snuffs with our generation out;
No matter, it's all one, it's but a name
Not as late honeysuckle half so stout;
So think upon it how the fire burns blue,
Its hottest, when the flame is all but spent;
Thank God the fuel is low, we'll not renew
That length of flame into our firmament;
Think too the rooftree crackles and will fall
On us, who saw the sacred fury's height—
Seated in her tall chair, with the black shawl
From head to foot, burning with motherly light
More spectral than November dusk could mix
With sunset, to blaze on her pale crucifix.

VIII

This message hastens lest we both go down
Scattered, with no character, to death;
Death is untutored, with an ignorant frown
For precious identities of breath.
But you perhaps will say confusion stood,
A vulture, near the heart of all our kin:
I've heard the echoes in a dark tangled wood
Yet never saw I a face peering within.
These evils being anonymities,
We fulminate, in exile from the earth,
Aged exclusions of blood memories—
Those superstitions of explosive birth;
Until there'll be of us not anything
But foolish death, who is confusion's king.

IX

Not power nor the casual hand of God
Shall keep us whole in our dissevering air,
It is a stink upon this pleasant sod
So foul, the hovering buzzard sees it fair;
I ask you will it end therefore tonight
And the moth tease again the windy flame,
Or spiders, eating their loves, hide in the night
At last, drowsy with self-devouring shame?
Call it the house of Atreus where we live—
Which one of us the Greek perplexed with crime
Questions the future: bring that lucid sieve
To strain the appointed particles of time!
Whether by Corinth or by Thebes we go
The way is brief, but the fixed doom, not so.

X

Captains of industry, your aimless power
Awakens harsh velleities of time:
Let you, brother, captaining your hour
Be zealous that your numbers are all prime,
Lest false division with sly mathematic
Plunder the inner mansion of the blood,
The Thracian, swollen with pride, besiege the Attic—
Invader foraging the sacred wood:
Yet the prime secret whose simplicity
Your towering engine hammers to reduce,
Though driven, holds that bulwark of the sea
Which breached will turn unspeaking fury loose
To drown out him who swears to rectify
Infinity, that has nor ear nor eye.

1931

The Wolves

There are wolves in the next room waiting
With heads bent low, thrust out, breathing
At nothing in the dark; between them and me
A white door patched with light from the hall
Where it seems never (so still is the house)
A man has walked from the front door to the stair.
It has all been forever. Beasts claw the floor.
I have brooded on angels and archfiends
But no man has ever sat where the next room's
Crowded with wolves, and for the honor of man
I affirm that never have I before. Now while
I have looked for the evening star at a cold window
And whistled when Arcturus spilt his light,
I've heard the wolves scuffle, and said: So this
Is man; so—what better conclusion is there—
The day will not follow night, and the heart
Of man has a little dignity, but less patience
Than a wolf's, and a duller sense that cannot
Smell its own mortality. (This and other
Meditations will be suited to other times
After dog silence howls his epitaph.)
Now remember courage, go to the door,
Open it and see whether coiled on the bed
Or cringing by the wall, a savage beast
Maybe with golden hair, with deep eyes
Like a bearded spider on a sunlit floor
Will snarl—and man can never be alone.

1931

The Anabasis

In Mem. L.N.L. Ob. MCMXXXII

Noble beyond degree
In a democracy:
Slight woman whose spent grace
Banishes their visiòn
To the thin trackless air,
Stop now upon the stair
As they have seen you do
Meridional and true,
And with nut-brown hair
Restore location
To them now blinded quite
By the grave's after-light,
For unless it be done
The slave heart all alone
Strives timelessly
To go where you are gone—
Whether to vaults of air,
Imponderable nowhere,
Or the reducing sea—
The regions that are fair
Beyond heart's mastery.
They try your form to see
(Its lineless agony)
In our philosophy
Which stops, as cold and bare
As headless hair,
As lifeless as your bones,
Obtuse as meadow stones:
Re-corporated be!
(They cry you in despair)
Lest we, a blind race,

Imitate mortality
For all our living's pace,
And drawn into the bliss
Of your dispersèd face
Should join, before our place,
Death's long anabasis.

1932

Brief Message

This, Warren, is our trouble now:
Not even fools could disavow
Three centuries of piety
Grown bare as a cottonwood tree
(A timber seldom drawn and sawn
And chiefly used to hang men on),
So face with calm that heritage
And earn contempt before the age.

1932

Inside and Outside

I

~~Now twenty-four or maybe twenty-five~~
Was the woman's age, and her white brow was sleek;
Lips parted in surprise, the flawless cheek;
The long brown hair coiled sullenly alive;
Her hands, dropt in her lap, could not arrive
At the novel on the table, being weak;
Nor breath, expunger of the mortal streak
Of nature, its own tenement contrive;

For look you how her body stiffly lies
Just as she left it, unprepared to stay,
The posture waiting on the sleeping eyes,
While the body's life, deep as a covered well,
Instinctive as the wind, busy as May,
Burns out a secret passageway to hell.

II

There is not anything to say to those
Speechless, who have stood up white to the eye
All night—till day, harrying the game too close,
Quarries the perils that at midnight lie
Waiting for those who hope to mortify
With foolish daylight their most anxious fear,
A bloodless and white fear that she may die
In the hushed room, and leave them soundless here:

There is no word that death can find to say
Deeper than life, savager than their time.
When Gabriel's trumpet ends all life's delay,
Will crash the beams of firmamental woe:
Not nature will sustain the even crime
Of death, though death sustains all nature, so.

1932

Ode to Fear

Variation on a Theme by Collins

Let the day glare: O memory, your tread
Beats to the pulse of suffocating night—
Night peering from his dark but fire-lit head
Burns on the day his tense and secret light.

Now they dare not to gloss your savage dream,
O beast of the heart, those saints who cursed your name;
You are the current of the frozen stream,
Shadow invisible, ambushed and vigilant flame.

My eldest companion present in solitude,
Watch-dog of Thebes when the blind hero strove:
You, omniscient, at the cross-roads stood
When Laius, the slain dotard, drenched the grove.

Now to the eye of prophecy immune,
Fading and harried, you stalk us in the street
From the recesses of the August noon,
Alert world over, crouched on the air's feet.

You are our surety to immortal life,
God's hatred of the universal stain—
The heritage, O Fear, of ancient strife
Compounded with the tissue of the vein.

And I when all is said have seen your form
Most agile and most treacherous to the world
When, on a child's long day, a dry storm
Burst on the cedars, lit by the sun and hurled!

1932

Records

At nine years a sickly boy lay down
At bedtime on a cot by mother's bed
And as the two darks merged the room became
So strange it left the boy half dead:

The boy-man on the Ox Road walked along
The man he was to be and yet another,
It seemed the grandfather of his mother,
In knee-breeches silver-buckled like a song,
His hair long and a cocked hat on his head,
A straight back and slow dignity for stride;
The road, red clay sun-cracked and baked,
Led fearlessly through scrub pines on each side
Hour after hour—the old road cracked and burned,
The trees countless, and his thirst unslaked.
Yet steadily with discipline like fate
Without memory, too ancient to be learned,
The man walked on and as if it were yesterday
Came easily to a two-barred gate
And stopped, and peering over a little way
He saw a dog-run country store fallen-in,
Deserted, but he said, 'Who's there?'
And then a tall fat man with stringy hair
And a manner that was innocent of sin,
His galluses greasy, his eyes coldly gray,
Appeared, and with a gravely learned air
Spoke from the deep coherence of hell—
The pines thundered, the sky blacked away,
The man in breeches, all knowledge in his stare,
A moment shuddered as the world fell.

II. A VISION

At twenty years the strong boy walked alone
Most fashionably dressed in the deserted park
At midnight, where the far lights burned low
And summer insects whined with little tone.
There was a final and comfortable dark
So that he walked deliberately slow;
It was not far from home, he'd been to see
His girl, who had sat silent and alone.
Picking his way upon the patched brick walk,
It being less dark near the street, he hastened
And knew a sense of fine immediacy
And then he heard some old forgotten talk
At a short distance like a hundred miles
Filling the air with its secrecy,
And was afraid of all the living air:
Now between steps with one heel lifted
A stern command froze him to the spot
And then a tall thin man with stringy hair,
Fear in his eyes, his breath quick and hot,
His arms lank and his neck a little twisted,
Spoke, and the trees sifted the air:
'I'm growing old,' he said, 'you have no choice,'
And said no more, but his bright eyes insisted
Incalculably with his relentless voice.

1932

The Traveller

To Archibald MacLeish

The afternoon with heavy hours
Lies vacant on the wanderer's sight
And sunset waits whose cloudy towers
Expect the legions of the night

Till sullen thunder from the cave
Of twilight with deliberate swell
Whispers the air his darkening slave
To loose the nether bolts of hell

To crush the battlements of cloud
The wall of light around the West
So that the swarming dark will crowd
The traveller upon his quest

And all the air with heavy hours
Sinks on the wanderer's dull sight
And the thick dark whose hidden towers
Menace his travel to the night

Rolls forward, backward hill to hill
Until the seeker knows not where
Beyond the shade of Peachers' Mill
In the burnt meadow, with colourless hair

The secret ones around a stone
Their lips withdrawn in meet surprise
Lie still, being naught but bone
With naught but space within their eyes

Until bewildered by the road
And half-forgetful of his quest
The wanderer with such a load
Of breathing, being too late a guest

Turns back, so near the secret stone,
Falls down breathless at last and blind,
And a dark shift within the bone
Brings him the end he could not find.

1932

Unnatural Love

Landor, not that I doubt your word,
That you had strove with none
At seventy-five and had deferred
To nature and art alone;
It is rather that at thirty-two
From us I see them part
After they served, so sweetly, you—
Yet nature has no heart:
Brother and sister are estranged
By his ambitious lies
For he his sister Helen much deranged—
Outraged her, and put coppers on her eyes.

1932

The Mediterranean

Quem das finem, rex magne, dolorum?

Where we went in the boat was a long bay
A slingshot wide, walled in by towering stone—
Peaked margin of antiquity's delay,
And we went there out of time's monotone:

Where we went in the black hull no light moved
But a gull white-winged along the feckless wave,
The breeze, unseen but fierce as a body loved,
That boat drove onward like a willing slave:

Where we went in the small ship the seaweed
Parted and gave to us the murmuring shore,
And we made feast and in our secret need
Devoured the very plates Aeneas bore:

Where derelict you see through the low twilight
The green coast that you, thunder-tossed, would win,
Drop sail, and hastening to drink all night
Eat dish and bowl to take that sweet land in!

Where we feasted and caroused on the sandless
Pebbles, affecting our day of piracy,
What prophecy of eaten plates could landless
Wanderers fulfil by the ancient sea?

We for that time might taste the famous age
Eternal here yet hidden from our eyes
When lust of power undid its stuffless rage;
They, in a wineskin, bore earth's paradise.

Let us lie down once more by the breathing side
Of Ocean, where our live forefathers sleep
As if the Known Sea still were a month wide—
Atlantis howls but is no longer steep!

What country shall we conquer, what fair land
Unman our conquest and locate our blood?
We've cracked the hemispheres with careless hand!
Now, from the Gates of Hercules we flood

Westward, westward till the barbarous brine
Whelms us to the tired land where tasseling corn,
Fat beans, grapes sweeter than muscadine
Rot on the vine: in that land were we born.

1933

Aeneas at Washington

I myself saw furious with blood
Neoptolemus, at his side the black Atridae,
Hecuba and the hundred daughters, Priam
Cut down, his filth drenching the holy fires.
In that extremity I bore me well,
A true gentleman, valorous in arms,
Disinterested and honourable. Then fled:
That was a time when civilization
Run by the few fell to the many, and
Crashed to the shout of men, the clang of arms:
Cold victualing I seized, I hoisted up
The old man my father upon my back,
In the smoke made by sea for a new world
Saving little—a mind imperishable
If time is, a love of past things tenuous
As the hesitation of receding love.

(To the reduction of uncitied littorals
We brought chiefly the vigor of prophecy,
Our hunger breeding calculation
And fixed triumphs.)

                              I saw the thirsty dove
In the glowing fields of Troy, hemp ripening
And tawny corn, the thickening Blue Grass
All lying rich forever in the green sun.
I see all things apart, the towers that men
Contrive I too contrived long, long ago.
Now I demand little. The singular passion
Abides its object and consumes desire
In the circling shadow of its appetite.

There was a time when the young eyes were slow,
Their flame steady beyond the firstling fire,
I stood in the rain, far from home at nightfall
By the Potomac, the great Dome lit the water,
The city my blood had built I knew no more
While the screech-owl whistled his new delight
Consecutively dark.

                    Stuck in the wet mire
Four thousand leagues from the ninth buried city
I thought of Troy, what we had built her for.

1933

Aeneas at New York

You have Sir said it well but I have if
Not knowledge a long memory of arms
The dates the various implements of war
Is it just to demand of us also to bear arms?
It is just: what manner of man was he
Sinon who swore at Neptune's priest, swearing
When the hard spear betrayed the horse's belly?
First we are priests second we are not whores
We are those who have arranged the auguries
And in dangerous youth made the good battle
I think Sir that you honoring our trade
(And nothing is lost save its honor)
And wishing us our own integrity and calm
Fall, if I may say it with respect, in error:
Is it just to demand of us also to bear arms
It is just and it is chiefly the nice question
Of the period of life and of whose arms:
You will remember the name of the poet fighting,
The young man at Salamis. Was he a whore?
The poet is he who fights on the passionate
Side and whoever loses he wins; when he
Is defeated it is hard to say who wins
Appreciation of victory contains no views
Neither views nor princes nor are there rules
There is the infallible instinct for the right battle
On the passionate side. With whose arms
Not arms of Mister J. P. Morgan: he is not one:

[A reply to Archibald MacLeish's poem, "Invocation to the Social Muse,"
in *The New Republic*, October 26, 1932]

With one's own arms when necessity detects
The fir-built horse inside the gates of Troy
We have nothing to do with Aulis nor intrigues
At Mycenae. I cannot of course prescribe
For other cities. Here (I merely suggest it)
Is what we did at Troy: there was no column
Of marchers there were myself and sad Hector
Have you Penates have you altars, have
You your great-great-grandfather's breeches?
Do not I do not attempt to wear the greaves
The moths are fed; our shanks too thin. Have you
His flintlock or had he none have you bought
A new Browning? The use of arms is ownership
Of the appropriate gun. It is ownership that brings
Victory that is not hinted at in "Das Kapital."
I think there is never but one true war
So let us as you desire perfect our trade.

The Ancestors

When the night's coming and the last light falls
A weak child among lost shadows on the floor,
It is your listening: pulse heeds the strain
Of fore and after, wind shivers the door.
What masterful delay commands the blood
Breaking its access to the living heart?
Consider this, the secret indecision,
Not rudeness of time but the systaltic flood
Of ancient failure begging its new start:
The flickered pause between the day and night
(When the heart knows its informality)
The bones hear but the eyes will never see—
Punctilious abyss, the yawn of space
Come once a day to suffocate the sight.
There is no man on earth who can be free
Of this, the eldest in the latest crime.

1933

Shadow and Shade

The shadow streamed into the wall—
The wall, break-shadow in the blast;
We lingered wordless while a tall
Shade enclouded the shadow's cast.

The torrent of the reaching shade
Broke shadow into all its parts,
What then had been of shadow made
Found exigence in fits and starts

Where nothing properly had name
Save that still element the air,
Burnt sea of universal frame
In which impounded now we were:

I took her hand, I shut her eyes
And all her shadow cleft with shade,
Shadow was crushed beyond disguise
But, being fear, was unafraid.

I asked fair shadow at my side:
What more shall fiery shade require?
We lay long in the immense tide
Of shade and shadowy desire

And saw the dusk assail the wall,
The black surge, mounting, crash the stone!
Companion of this lust, we fall,
I said, lest we should die alone.

1933

The Meaning of Life

A Monologue

Think about it at will: there is that
Which is the commentary; there's that other,
Which may be called the immaculate
Conception of its essence in itself.
It is necessary to distinguish the weights
Of the two methods lest the first smother
The second, the second be speechless (without the first).
I was saying this more briefly the other day
But one must be explicit as well as brief.
When I was a small boy I lived at home
For nine years in that part of old Kentucky
Where the mountains fringe the Blue Grass,
The old men shot at one another for luck;
It made me think I was like none of them.
At twelve I was determined to shoot only
For honor; at twenty not to shoot at all;
I know at thirty-three that one must shoot
As often as one gets the rare chance—
In killing there is more than commentary.
One's sense of the proper decoration alters
But there's a kind of lust feeds on itself
Unspoken to, unspeaking; subterranean
As a black river full of eyeless fish
Heavy with spawn; with a passion for time
Longer than the arteries of a cave.

1933

The Meaning of Death

An After-Dinner Speech

I rise, gentlemen, it is the pleasant hour.
Darkness falls. The night falls.

                           Time, fall no more.
Let that be life—time falls no more. The threat
Of time we in our own courage have forsworn.
Let light fall, there shall be eternal light
And all the light shall on our heads be worn

Although at evening clouds infest the sky
Broken at base from which the lemon sun
Pours acid of winter on a useful view—
Four water-towers, two churches, and a river:
These are the sights I give in to at night
When the long covers loose the roving eye
To find the horror of the day a shape
Of life: we would have more than living sight.
Past delusions are seen as if it all
Were yesterday flooded with lemon light,
Vice and virtue, hard sacrifice and crime
In the cold vanity of time.

                      Tomorrow
The landscape will respond to jocund day,
Bright roofs will scintillate with hues of May
And Phoebus' car, his daily circuit run,
Brings me to the year when, my time begun,
I loitered in the backyard by the alley;
When I was a small boy living at home
The dark came on in summer at eight o'clock
For Little Lord Fauntleroy in a perfect frock

By the alley: mother took him by the ear
To teach of the mixed modes an ancient fear.
Forgive me if I am personal.

Gentlemen, let's
Forget the past, its related errors, coarseness
Of parents, laxities, unrealities of principle.
Think of tomorrow. Make a firm postulate
Of simplicity in desire and act
Founded on the best hypotheses;
Desire to eat secretly, alone, lest
Ritual corrupt our charity,
Lest darkness fall and time fall
In a long night when learned arteries
Mounting the ice and sum of barbarous time
Shall yield, without essence, perfect accident.

We are the eyelids of defeated caves.

1934

Fragment of a Meditation

Not yet the thirtieth year, the thirtieth
Station where time reverses his light heels
To run both ways, and makes of forward back;
Whose long co-ordinates are birth and death
And zero is the origin of breath:
Not yet the thirtieth year of gratitude,
Not yet suffering but a year's lack,
All thanks that mid-mortality is done,
That the new breath on the invisible track
Winds anciently into my father's blood.

In the beginning the irresponsible Verb
Connived with chaos whence I've seen it start
Riddles in the head for the nervous heart
To count its beat on: all beginnings run
Like water the easiest way or like birds
Fly on their cool imponderable flood.

Then suddenly the noon turns afternoon
And afternoon like an ill-written page
Will fade, until the very stain of light
Gathers in all the venom of the night—
The equilibrium of the thirtieth age.

The thirtieth, not yet the thirtieth year
Of wonders, revelations, whispers, signs:
Impartial dumb truths of sound and sight
Known beyond speech, immune to common fear.
Already the wind whistles the revelations
Of the time, but I'll go back seventy years
And more to the great Administrations:
Yet six had gone and all the public men

Whom doctrine and an evil nature made
Were only errand boys beaten by the sun
While Henry Adams fuddled in the shade.

I've heard what they said, in the running tap
Drawing water, their watery words, clear
Like a sad harlot's useless lucid pap
(I've heard the lion of S Street get his cheer),
I understood it, the general syllable
In a private ear, lost. . . .

                        For who can tell
What the goat calls to the heifer, or the hen
Even to the cock her love? At thirty years
The years of the Christ, one will perceive, know,
Report new verity with a certain pen.

In the decade from eighteen-fifty-one
Where was Calhoun whose bristled intellect
Sumner the refined one did not admire?
I am convinced 'twas Calhoun who divined
How the great western star's last race would run
Unbridled round our personal defect,
Grinding its ash with engines of its mind.
'Too Southern and too simple,' his death's head
Uttered a *Dies Irae* that last day
When Senator Mason in a voice to stun
Read off his speech; then put Calhoun to bed.
They put him in his grave. Does the worm say
In the close senate of tempestuous clay
That his intellect makes too difficult
The grave, as his enemies our life?
It's quiet there, for the worm's one fault
Is not discourtesy (give worms their dues)
In case the guest hurried by mortal strife
Enter the house in muddy overshoes.

It was a time of tributes; let me pay
Tribute to a man grandfather knew well
(Or so 'twas said, but one can never tell),
A stocky man but slight, no symmetry
Of face and eye, yet a distinction
Of the poet against the world; he dreamed the soul
Of the wide world and prodigies to come;
Exemplar of dignity, a gentleman
Who raised the black flag of the lower mind;
Hated in life by all; in death praised;
I cannot yet begin to understand
Why we are proud that an ancestor knew
The crazy Poe, who was not of our kind—
Bats in the belfry that round and round flew
In vapors not quite wholesome for the mind.

After Calhoun the local tenements
Of nature, tempered to the exigencies
Of air and fire, blurred with the public sense,
Diffused, while the Black Republicans
Took a short memory to their hot desire,
And honor turned a common entity
Crying decisions from the evening news.
Yet in a year, at thirty, one shall see
The wisdom of history, how she takes
Each epoch by the neck and, growling, shakes
It like a rat while she faintly mews.
Perhaps at the age of thirty one shall see
In the wide world the prodigies to come:
The long-gestating Christ, the Agnulus
Of time, got in the belly of Abstraction
By Ambition, a bull of pious use.

O Pasiphaë! mother of god, lest nature,
Peritonitis or morning sickness stunt
The growth of god in an unwholesome juice,
Eat cannon and cornflakes, that the lamb,
Spaceless as snow, may spare the rational earth
(Weary of prodigies and the Holy Runt)
A second prodigious, two-legged birth.

The signs and portents screaming in the air,
The nativity in my thirtieth year
Will glow in the heavens, the myriad fireflies
At the holy hour hovering round the house
Will stream in the night like flaming hair,
And man will scurry with averted eyes
Crouching, peering, silent, a drunken mouse.
The orange groves will blossom, the shining Sierras
Kindle all night far as Los Angeles;
With a noise, threatening, of wandering bees
Coming, angry with the air of their carouse,
The lamb through the sandpaper gates of life
(Made rougher by the bull's intenser strife)
Will leap, while the wild-eyed Pasiphaë
By the inscrutable wrath of glory stung
Hears the Wise Men* come swiftly from the sea.
The bull smoothly rolls his powerful tongue.

1935

*I originally thought of the Wise Men as Mr. Herbert Hoover, the late Otto H. Kahn (American banker and philanthropist), and the late Gertrude Stein; but I decided that the occasion required even wiser persons than these; and when I couldn't find them, I gave it up, and brought the poem to an abrupt end.—A.T.

To the Romantic Traditionists

I have looked at them long,
My eyes blur; sourceless light
Keeps them forever young
Before our ageing sight.

You see them too—strict forms
Of will, the secret dignity
Of our dissolute storms;
They grow too bright to be.

What were they like? What mark
Can signify their charm?
They never saw the dark;
Rigid, they never knew alarm.

Do not the scene rehearse!
The perfect eyes enjoin
A contemptuous verse;
We speak the crabbed line.

Immaculate race! to yield
Us final knowledge set
In a cold frieze, a field
Of war but no blood let.

Are they quite willing,
Do they ask to pose,
Naked and simple, chilling
The very wind's nose?

They ask us how to live!
We answer: Again try
Being the drops we sieve.
What death it is to die!

Therefore because they nod,
Being too full of us,
I look at the turned sod
Where it is perilous

And yawning all the same
As if we knew them not
And history had no name—
No need to name the spot!

1935

The Ivory Tower

Let us begin to understand the argument.
There is a solution to everything: Science.
Separate those evils strictly social
From other evils that are eventually social.
It ends in all evils being social: Deduction.
Is not marriage a social institution,
Un contrat social? Is not prostitution
An institution? Abolish (1) marriage, (2) poverty.
We understand everything: Dialectic.
We who get plenty to eat and get it
Advertising the starvation of others
Understand everything not including
Ourselves: we have enough to eat. Oedipus
Was necessarily an example—everything
Is an example—of capitalism pooped
By decay; King Lear, of neurotic senility
Bred of tyrannous escape from reality;
Cleopatra, of the unadjusted girl.
Everybody but us is an example of capitalism.
We are understanding the argument
That we have got to make men slaves
Of their bellies in order to get them fed.

The sole problem is the problem of hunger
(Or the distribution of commodities)
And a beast came out of the sea
And a fire came out of the night
To them that were not hungry
The commodities being well distributed
And the prostate thrives a little, then delays,
The hour of light is brief, then decays;

But light must be a social institution
Even if we are not sure what the other
Is (*pro*, forth; *stare*, to stand).
We know everything to know on sea or land.
And on the mountains by the sea
There was enacted tragedy
(Or maybe in a hollow by a tree),
Both man and woman were well-fed
When he had brought her hot to bed
But he was largely make-believe
And she no better than a sieve.
Soon the uneconomic woe
That love engenders crushed them, so
That every time they drank or ate
They cursed the board where food was set.

Axel's Castle, the text they took,
Was a most remarkable book
But yet in spite of Mr. Wilson
Beef and cheese washed down by Pilsen
Did not adjust the sexual act
To truths of economic fact,
So was produced this tragedy
In a far tower of ivory
Where, O young men, late in the night
All you who drink light and stroke the air
Come back, seeking the night, and cry
To strict Rapunzel to let down her hair.

1936

To the Lacedemonians

An old soldier on the night before the veterans' reunion talks partly to himself, partly to imaginary comrades:

The people—people of my kind, my own
People but strange with a white light
In the face: the streets hard with motion
And the hard eyes that look one way.
Listen! the high whining tone
Of the motors, I hear the dull commotion:
I am come, a child in an old play.

I am here with a secret in the night;
Because I am here the dead wear gray.

It is a privilege to be dead; for you
Cannot know what absence is nor seize
The odour of pure distance until
From you, slowly dying in the head,
All sights and sounds of the moment, all
The life of sweet intimacy shall fall
Like a swift at dusk.

          Sheer time! Stroke of the heart
Towards retirement. . . .

          Gentlemen, my secret is
Damnation: where have they, the citizens, all
Come from? They were not born in my father's
House, nor in their fathers': on a street corner
By motion sired, not born; by rest dismayed.
The tempest will unwind—the hurricane
Consider, knowing its end, the headlong pace?

I have watched it and endured it, I have delayed
Judgment: it warn't in my time, by God, so
That the mere breed absorbed the generation!

Yet I, hollow head, do see but little;
Old man: no memory: aimless distractions.

I was a boy, I never knew cessation
Of the bright course of blood along the vein;
Moved, an old dog by me, to field and stream
In the speaking ease of the fall rain;
When I was a boy the light on the hills
Was there because I could see it, not because
Some special gift of God had put it there.
Men expect too much, do too little,
Put the contraption before the accomplishment,
Lack skill of the interior mind
To fashion dignity with shapes of air.
Luxury, yes—but not elegance!
Where have they come from?

                     Go you tell them
That we their servants, well-trained, gray-coated
Gray-haired (both foot and horse) or in
The grave, them obey . . . obey them,
What commands?

           My father said
That everything but kin was less than kind.
The young men like swine argue for a rind,
A flimsy shell to put their weakness in;
Will-less, ruled by what they cannot see;
Hunched like savages in a rotten tree
They wait for the thunder to speak: Union!
That joins their separate fear.

                        I fought
But did not care; a leg shot off at Bethel,
Given up for dead; but knew neither shell-shock
Nor any self-indulgence. Well may war be
Terrible to those who have nothing to gain
For the illumination of the sense:
When the peace is a trade route, figures
For the budget, reduction of population,
Life grown sullen and immense
Lusts after immunity to pain.

There is no civilization without death;
There is now the wind for breath.

Waken, lords and ladies gay, we cried,
And marched to Cedar Run and Malvern Hill,
Kinsmen and friends from Texas to the Tide—
Vain chivalry of the personal will!

Waken, we shouted, lords and ladies gay,
We go to win the precincts of the light,
Unshadowing restriction of our day . . . .
Regard now, in the seventy years of night,

Them, the young men who watch us from the curbs:
They hold the glaze of wonder in their stare—
Our crooked backs, hands fetid as old herbs,
The tallow eyes, wax face, the foreign hair!

Soldiers, march! we shall not fight again
The Yankees with our guns well-aimed and rammed—
All are born Yankees of the race of men
And this, too, now the country of the damned:

Poor bodies crowding round us! The white face
Eyeless with eyesight only, the modern power—
Huddled sublimities of time and space,
They are the echoes of a raging tower

That reared its moment upon a gone land,
Pouring a long cold wrath into the mind—
Damned souls, running the way of sand
Into the destination of the wind!

1932/1936

Pastoral

The enquiring fields, courtesies
And tribulations of the air—
Be still and give them peace:

The girl in the gold hair
With her young man in clover
In shadow of the day's glare

And there they were by the river
Where a leaf's light interval
Ringed the deep hurrying mirror;

Yet naught there to befall
Such meditations as beguile
Courage when love grows tall

For tall he was in green style
Of a willow shaking the pool.
'Let time be quiet as a mile,'

He said, 'time is love's fool.'
Yet time he would appease:
'Time, be easy and cool.'

The enquiring courtesies
Of first dusk then debated
To cloud their agonies:

She, her head back, waited
Barbarous the stalking tide;
He, nor balked nor sated

But plunged into the wide
Area of mental ire,
Lay at her wandering side.

1936

Cold Pastoral

Walk in this faithless grass with studious tread,
Lest mice, weasels, germane beasts, too soon
The tall hat and eyes, the fierce feet, for dead
Descry, and fix you prone in their revelling moon.

Walk, call to the first peewit that hops
Like a quotation from old access to joy,
And say: 'Have you nipped the friendly bud that drops
False liquors to the quick heart I employ?

'Have you seen the dew? Perhaps the blushed moss
That begs the hateful spring one month away?
And what of hounds—sniffing as though to gloss
The utterance of worms in ecstasy?

'You have seen something, bird, but you will talk
Idiocy here: go away. What of the city
Full of night air and traffic—what of these, as I walk
Repeated grass with all its single pity?'

Walk in this grass, I say, as if you touched
The roots of grass with fearful cozenage.
Advice you take from me comes to you crutched
Like a beggar—youth zealous for old age.

1936

The Robber Bridegroom

Turn back. Turn, young lady dear
A murderer's house you enter here

I was wooed and won little bird

(I have watched them come bright girls
Out of the rising sun, with curls)
The stair is tall the cellar deep
The wind coughs in the halls

I never wish to sleep

From the ceiling the sky falls
It will press you and press you, dear.

It is my desire to fear

(What a child! she desires her fear)
The house is whirling night, the guests
Grains of dust from the northwest

I do not come for rest

There is no rest for the dead

Ready for the couch of my groom

In a long room beneath the dew
Where the walls embrace and cling.

I wear my wedding ring

He will cut off your finger
And the blood will linger

Little bird!

1936

Eclogue of the Liberal and the Poet

LIBERAL

In that place, shepherd, all the men are dead.

POET

Yes, look at the water grim and black
Where immense Europa rears her head,
Her face pinched and her breasts slack.

LIBERAL

I said, shepherd, all the men are dead.

POET

Shall I turn to the road that goes America?
Is that a place for men to be dead
Or living? If you don't mind being asked.

LIBERAL

Try it and see. It's a pretty good way
To skim three thousand miles in a day
And none of them America.

POET

But what about her face and the tasked
Wonders of her air and soil, her big belly
That Putnam writes about under the sun?

LIBERAL

I don't know Put, I don't know his Nelly—
I'd name her that if she'd name it fun
But you know she hasn't any name,
Nowhere you touch her she's the same.

POET

What, shepherd, are we talking about?

LIBERAL

You started it, shepherd.

POET

Shepherd, I didn't.

LIBERAL

You did; you saw the poetical face of Europe.

POET

You said it was no place for men to be.

LIBERAL

I meant seawater; you thought I meant hope.

POET

Hell, I reckon you think I am a dope.

LIBERAL

I didn't say that; I said there was no place.

POET

If not in a place, where are the People weeping?

LIBERAL

They creep weeping in the face, not place.

POET

Is it something with which we may cope—
The weeping, the creeping, the peepee-ing, the peeping?

LIBERAL

Hanging is something which I will do with this rope.

POET

Alas, for us who peep, weeping,
Alas, for us you see but little hope.

LIBERAL

Alas, I didn't say that; you rhymed hope with rope.
I meant I was going to hang us both for creeping.

POET

Afterwards they could process us into soap;
Afterwards they would rhyme soap with hope.

BOTH

What a cheerful rhyme! Clean not mean!
Been not seen! Not tired—expired!
We must now decide about place.
We decide that place is the big weeping face
And the other abstract lace of the race.

LIBERAL

Shepherd, what are we talking about?

POET

Oh, why, shepherd, are we stalking about?

1938

The Trout Map

The Management Area of Cherokee
National Forest, interested in fish,
Has mapped Tellico and Bald Rivers
And North River, with the tributaries
Brookshire Branch and Sugar Cove Creek:
A fishy map for facile fishery

In Marvel's kind Ocean: drawn in two
Colors, blue and red—blue for the hue
Of Europe (Tennessee water is green),
Red lines by blue streams to warn
The fancy-fishmen from protected fish;
Black borders hold the Area in a cracked dish,

While other blacks, the dots and dashes, wire
The fisher's will through classic laurel
Over boar tracks to creamy pot-holes lying
Under Bald falls that thump the shying
Trout: we flew Professor, the Hackles and Worms.
(Tom Bagley and I were dotted and dashed wills.)

Up Green Cove gap from Preacher Millsap's cabin
We walked a confident hour of victory,
Sloped to the west on a trail that led us
To Bald River where map and scene were one
In seen-identity. Eight trout is the story
In three miles. We came to a rock-bridge

On which the road went left around a hill,
The river, right, tumbled into a cove;
But the map dashed the road along the stream
And we dotted man's fishiest enthymeme
With jellied feet upon understanding love
Of what eyes see not, that nourishes the will:

We were fishers, weren't we? And tried to fish
The egoed belly's dry cartograph—
Which made the government fish lie down and laugh.
(Tommy and I listened, we heard them shake
Mountain and cove because the map was fake.)
After eighteen miles our feet were clownish,

Then darkness took us into wheezing straits
Where coarse Magellan idling with his fates
Ran with the gulls for map around the Horn,
Or wheresoever the mind with tidy scorn
Revisits the world upon a dry sunbeam.
Now mapless the mountains were a dream.

1939

PART THREE

Jubilo

To Arthur Mizener

Hit mus' be now de Kingdom comin'
And de year of Jubilo . . .

Tail-spinning from the shelves of sky
See how it dips and tacks and tosses
To cast a beam in the mind's eye:
Who will count the gains and the losses
    On the Day of Jubilo?

Public accountant with double entry
Enter in red war's final cast
In the black column the pacing sentry,
Old women picking the hogs' mast
    For the Day of Jubilo

Lean to the crowded air and hear,
Eavesdropper, how it goes inside
Your own deaf and roaring ear:
Boys caress the machines they ride
    On the Day of Jubilo

After the dry and sticking tongue
After our incivility
Who will inflate the poet's lung
Gone flat of this indignity
    Till the Day of Jubilo?

Scholar, no dog will have your day
For all your capital's run out,
Wry baby in wet disarray—
Scholar, prepare your meagre clout
    For the Day of Jubilo

Under the slip and slide of day
Think, at the end you'll never be
Trapped in a fox-hole of decay
Nor snip nor glide of history
    After the Day of Jubilo

All our jubilant eyes are raised,
Jubilo. Over the barbican
On the great Day pure and dazed,
Empty of heart the empty man
    Of the Day of Jubilo

Then for the Day of Jubilo
The patient bares his arm at dawn
To suck the blood's transfusing glow
And then when all the blood is gone
    (For the Day of Jubilo)

Salt serum stays his arteries
Sly tide threading the ribs of sand,
Till his lost being dries, and cries
For that unspeakable salt land
    Beyond the Day of Jubilo.

1943

Sonnets at Christmas

I

This is the day His hour of life draws near,
Let me get ready from head to foot for it
Most handily with eyes to pick the year
For small feed to reward a feathered wit.
Some men would see it an epiphany
At ease, at food and drink, others at chase;
Yet I, stung lassitude, with ecstasy
Unspent argue the season's difficult case
So: Man, dull creature of enormous head,
What would he look at in the coiling sky?
But I must kneel again unto the Dead
While Christmas bells of paper white and red,
Figured with boys and girls spilt from a sled,
Ring out the silence I am nourished by.

II

Ah, Christ, I love you rings to the wild sky
And I must think a little of the past:
When I was ten I told a stinking lie
That got a black boy whipped; but now at last
The going years, caught in an after-glow,
Reverse like balls englished upon green baize—
Let them return, let the round trumpets blow
The ancient crackle of the Christ's deep gaze.
Deafened and blind, with senses yet unfound,
Am I, untutored to the after-wit
Of knowledge, knowing a nightmare has no sound;
Therefore with idle hands and head I sit
In late December before the fire's daze
Punished by crimes of which I would be quit.

1934

More Sonnets at Christmas

To the memory of Denis Devlin

I

Again the native hour lets down the locks
Uncombed and black, but gray the bobbing beard;
Ten years ago His eyes, fierce shuttlecocks,
Pierced the close net of what I failed: I feared
The belly-cold, the grave-clout, that betrayed
Me dithering in the drift of cordial seas;
Ten years are time enough to be dismayed
By mummy Christ, head crammed between his knees.

Suppose I take an arrogant bomber, stroke
By stroke, up to the frazzled sun to hear
Sun-ghostlings whisper: Yes, the capital yoke—
Remove it and there's not a ghost to fear
This crucial day, whose decapitate joke
Languidly winds into the inner ear.

II

The day's at end and there's nowhere to go,
Draw to the fire, even this fire is dying;
Get up and once again politely lying
Invite the ladies toward the mistletoe
With greedy eyes that stare like an old crow.
How pleasantly the holly wreaths did hang
And how stuffed Santa did his reindeer clang
Above the golden oaken mantel, years ago!

Then hang this picture for a calendar,
As sheep for goat, and pray most fixedly
For the cold martial progress of your star,
With thoughts of commerce and society,
Well-milked Chinese, Negroes who cannot sing,
The Huns gelded and feeding in a ring.

III

Give me this day a faith not personal
As follows: The American people fully armed
With assurance policies, righteous and harmed,
Battle the world of which they're not at all.
That lying boy of ten who stood in the hall,
His hat in hand (thus by his father charmed:
'You may be President'), was not alarmed
Nor even left uneasy by his fall.

Nobody said that he could be a plumber,
Carpenter, clerk, bus-driver, bombardier;
Let little boys go into violent slumber,
Aegean squall and squalor where their fear
Is of an enemy in remote oceans
Unstalked by Christ: these are the better notions.

IV

Gay citizen, myself, and thoughtful friend,
Your ghosts are Plato's Christians in the cave.
Unfix your necks, turn to the door; the nave
Gives back the cheated and light dividend
So long sequestered; now, new-rich, you'll spend
Flesh for reality inside a stone
Whose light obstruction, like a gossamer bone,
Dead or still living, will not break or bend.

Thus light, your flesh made pale and sinister
And put off like a dog that's had his day,
You will be Plato's kept philosopher,
Albino man bleached from the mortal clay,
Mild-mannered, gifted in your master's ease
While the sun squats upon the waveless seas.

1942

Ode to Our Young Pro-consuls of the Air

To St.-John Perse

Once more the country calls
From sleep, as from his doom,
    Each citizen to take
    His modest stake
Where the sky falls
With a Pacific boom.

Warm winds in even climes
Push southward angry bees
    As we, with tank and plane,
    Wrest land and main
From yellow mimes,
The puny Japanese.

Boys hide in lunging cubes
Crouching to explode,
    Beyond Atlantic skies,
    With cheerful cries
Their barking tubes
Upon the German toad.

Marvelling day by day
Upon the human kind
    What might I have done
    (A poet alone)
To balk or slay
These enemies of mind?

I sought by night to foal
Chimeras into men—
  Decadence of power
  That, at late hour,
Untimed the soul
To live the past again:

Toy sword, three-cornered hat
At York and Lexington—
  While *Bon-Homme* whipped at sea
  This enemy
Whose roar went flat
After George made him run;

Toy rifle, leather hat
Above the boyish beard—
  And in that Blue renown
  The Gray went down,
Down like a rat,
And even the rats cheered.

In a much later age
(Europe had been in flames)
  Proud Wilson yielded ground
  To franc and pound,
Made pilgrimage
In the wake of Henry James.

Where Lou Quatorze held *fête*
For sixty thousand men,
  France took the German sword
  But later, bored,
Opened the gate
To Hitler—at Compiègne.

In this bad time no part
The poet took, nor chance:
    He studied Swift and Donne,
    Ignored the Hun,
While with faint heart
Proust caused the fall of France.

Sad day at Oahu
When the Jap beetle hit!
    Our Proustian retort
    Was Kimmel and Short,
Old women in blue,
And then the beetle bit.

It was defeat, or near it!
Yet all that feeble time
    Brave Brooks and lithe MacLeish
    Had sworn to thresh
Our flagging spirit
With literature made Prime!

Cow Creek and bright Bear Wallow,
Nursing the blague that dulls
    Spirits grown Eliotic,
    Now patriotic
Are: we follow
The Irresponsibles!

Young men, Americans!
You go to win the world
    With zeal pro-consular
    For our whole star—
You partisans
Of liberty unfurled!

O animal excellence,
Take pterodactyl flight
      Fire-winged into the air
      And find your lair
With cunning sense
On some Arabian bight

Or sleep your dreamless sleep
(Reptilian bomber!) by
      The Mediterranean
      And like a man
Swear you to keep
Faith with imperial eye:

Take off, O gentle youth,
And coasting India
      Scale crusty Everest
      Whose mythic crest
Resists your truth;
And spying far away

Upon the Tibetan plain
A limping caravan,
      Dive, and exterminate
      The Lama, late
Survival of old pain.
Go kill the dying swan.

1943

Winter Mask

To the memory of W. B. Yeats

I

Towards nightfall when the wind
Tries the eaves and casements
(A winter wind of the mind
Long gathering its will)
I lay the mind's contents
Bare, as upon a table,
And ask, in a time of war,
Whether there is still
To a mind frivolously dull
Anything worth living for.

II

If I am meek and dull
And a poor sacrifice
Of perverse will to cull
The act from the attempt,
Just look into damned eyes
And give the returning glare;
For the damned like it, the more
Damnation is exempt
From what would save its heir
With a thing worth living for.

III

The poisoned rat in the wall
Cuts through the wall like a knife,
Then blind, drying, and small
And driven to cold water,
Dies of the water of life:

Both damned in eternal ice,
The traitor become the boor
Who had led his friend to slaughter,
Now bites his head—not nice,
The food that he lives for.

IV

I supposed two scenes of hell,
Two human bestiaries,
Might uncommonly well
Convey the doom I thought;
But lest the horror freeze
The gentler estimation
I go to the sylvan door
Where nature has been bought
In rational proration
As a thing worth living for.

V

Should the buyer have been beware?
It is an uneven trade
For man has wet his hair
Under the winter weather
With only fog for shade:
His mouth a bracketed hole
Picked by the crows that bore
Nature to their hanged brother,
Who rattles against the bole
The thing that he lived for.

I asked the master Yeats
Whose great style could not tell
Why it is man hates
His own salvation,
Prefers the way to hell,
And finds his last safety
In the self-made curse that bore
Him towards damnation:
The drowned undrowned by the sea,
The sea worth living for.

1942

Seasons of the Soul

To the memory of John Peale Bishop, 1892–1944

Allor porsi la mano un poco avante,
e colsi un ramicel da un gran pruno;
e il tronco suo gridò: Perchè mi schiante?

I. SUMMER

Summer, this is our flesh,
The body you let mature;
If now while the body is fresh
You take it, shall we give
The heart, lest heart endure
The mind's tattering
Blow of greedy claws?
Shall mind itself still live
If like a hunting king
It falls to the lion's jaws?

Under the summer's blast
The soul cannot endure
Unless by sleight or fast
It seize or deny its day
To make the eye secure.
Brothers-in-arms, remember
The hot wind dries and draws
With circular delay
The flesh, ash from the ember,
Into the summer's jaws.

It was a gentle sun
When, at the June solstice
Green France was overrun
With caterpillar feet.
No head knows where its rest is
Or may lie down with reason
When war's usurping claws
Shall take the heart escheat—
Green field in burning season
To stain the weevil's jaws.

The southern summer dies
Evenly in the fall:
We raise our tired eyes
Into a sky of glass,
Blue, empty, and tall
Without tail or head
Where burn the equal laws
For Balaam and his ass
Above the invalid dead,
Who cannot lift their jaws.

When was it that the summer
(Daylong a liquid light)
And a child, the new-comer,
Bathed in the same green spray,
Could neither guess the night?
The summer had no reason;
Then, like a primal cause
It had its timeless day
Before it kept the season
Of time's engaging jaws.

Two men of our summer world
Descended winding hell
And when their shadows curled
They fearfully confounded
The vast concluding shell:
Stopping, they saw in the narrow
Light a centaur pause
And gaze, then his astounded
Beard, with a notched arrow,
Part back upon his jaws.

II. AUTUMN

It had an autumn smell
And that was how I knew
That I was down a well:
I was no longer young;
My lips were numb and blue,
The air was like fine sand
In a butcher's stall
Or pumice to the tongue:
And when I raised my hand
I stood in the empty hall.

The round ceiling was high
And the gray light like shale
Thin, crumbling, and dry:
No rug on the bare floor
Nor any carved detail
To which the eye could glide;
I counted along the wall
Door after closed door
Through which a shade might slide
To the cold and empty hall.

I will leave this house, I said,
There is the autumn weather—
Here, nor living nor dead;
The lights burn in the town
Where men fear together.
Then on the bare floor,
But tiptoe lest I fall,
I walked years down
Towards the front door
At the end of the empty hall.

The door was false—no key
Or lock, and I was caught
In the house; yet I could see
I had been born to it
For miles of running brought
Me back where I began.
I saw now in the wall
A door open a slit
And a fat grizzled man
Come out into the hall:

As in a moonlit street
Men meeting are too shy
To check their hurried feet
But raise their eyes and squint
As through a needle's eye
Into the faceless gloom,—
My father in a gray shawl
Gave me an unseeing glint
And entered another room!
I stood in the empty hall

And watched them come and go
From one room to another,
Old men, old women—slow,
Familiar; girls, boys;
I saw my downcast mother
Clad in her street-clothes,
Her blue eyes long and small,
Who had no look or voice
For him whose vision froze
Him in the empty hall.

III. WINTER

Goddess sea-born and bright,
Return into the sea
Where eddying twilight
Gathers upon your people—
Cold goddess, hear our plea!
Leave the burnt earth, Venus,
For the drying God above,
Hanged in his windy steeple,
No longer bears for us
The living wound of love.

All the sea-gods are dead.
You, Venus, come home
To your salt maidenhead,
The tossed anonymous sea
Under shuddering foam—
Shade for lovers, where
A shark swift as your dove
Shall pace our company
All night to nudge and tear
The livid wound of love.

And now the winter sea:
Within her hollow rind
What sleek facility
Of sea-conceited scop
To plumb the nether mind!
Eternal winters blow
Shivering flakes, and shove
Bodies that wheel and drop—
Cold soot upon the snow
Their livid wound of love.

Beyond the undertow
The gray sea-foliage
Transpires a phosphor glow
Into the circular miles:
In the centre of his cage
The pacing animal
Surveys the jungle cove
And slicks his slithering wiles
To turn the venereal awl
In the livid wound of love.

Beyond the undertow
The rigid madrepore
Resists the winter's flow—
Headless, unageing oak
That gives the leaf no more.
Wilfully as I stood
Within the thickest grove
I seized a branch, which broke;
I heard the speaking blood
(From the livid wound of love)

Drip down upon my toe:
'We are the men who died
Of self-inflicted woe,
Lovers whose stratagem
Led to their suicide.'
I touched my sanguine hair
And felt it drip above
Their brother who, like them,
Was maimed and did not bear
The living wound of love.

IV. SPRING

Irritable spring, infuse
Into the burning breast
Your combustible juice
That as a liquid soul
Shall be the body's guest
Who lights, but cannot stay
To comfort this unease
Which, like a dying coal,
Hastens the cooler day
Of the mother of silences.

Back in my native prime
I saw the orient corn
All space but no time,
Reaching for the sun
Of the land where I was born:
It was a pleasant land
Where even death could please
Us with an ancient pun—
All dying for the hand
Of the mother of silences.

In time of bloody war
Who will know the time?
Is it a new spring star
Within the timing chill,
Talking, or just a mime,
That rises in the blood—
Thin Jack-and-Jilling seas
Without the human will?
Its light is at the flood,
Mother of silences!

It burns us each alone
Whose burning arrogance
Burns up the rolling stone,
This earth—Platonic cave
Of vertiginous chance!
Come, tired Sisyphus,
Cover the cave's egress
Where light reveals the slave,
Who rests when sleeps with us
The mother of silences.

Come, old woman, save
Your sons who have gone down
Into the burning cave:
Come, mother, and lean
At the window with your son
And gaze through its light frame
These fifteen centuries
Upon the shirking scene
Where men, blind, go lame:
Then, mother of silences,

Speak, that we may hear;
Listen, while we confess
That we conceal our fear;
Regard us, while the eye
Discerns by sight or guess
Whether, as sheep foregather
Upon their crooked knees,
We have begun to die;
Whether your kindness, mother,
Is mother of silences.

1944

The Eye

λαιδρὴ κορώνη, κῶς τὸ χεῖλος οὐκ ἀλγεῖς—Callimachus

To the memory of E. E. Cummings

I see the horses and the sad streets
Of my childhood in an agate eye
Roving, under the clean sheets,
Over a black hole in the sky.

The ill man becomes the child,
The evil man becomes the lover;
The natural man with evil roiled
Pulls down the sphereless sky for cover.

I see the gray heroes and the graves
Of my childhood in the nuclear eye—
Horizons spent in dun caves
Sucked down into the sinking sky.

The happy child becomes the man,
The elegant man becomes the mind,
The fathered gentleman who can
Perform quick feats of gentle kind.

I see the long field and the noon
Of my childhood in the carbolic eye,
Dissolving pupil of the moon
Seared from the raveled hole of the sky.

The nice ladies and gentlemen,
The teaser and the jelly-bean
Play cockalorum-and-the-hen,
When the cool afternoons pour green:

I see the father and the cooling cup
Of my childhood in the swallowing sky
Down, down, until down is up
And there is nothing in the eye,

Shut shutter of the mineral man
Who takes the fatherless dark to bed,
The acid sky to the brain-pan;
And calls the crows to peck his head.

1948

Two Conceits

for the Eye to Sing, if Possible

I

SING a song of 'sistence
    Pocket full of Eye
Two billion Turtle-doves
    Mourning in a sty
When the sty was open
    The Doves began to sing
Wasn't it a stylish dish
    To Turtle-doves to fling

Sing a song of Agapé
    Loving's in the I
Two billion Messieurs Gide
    Drinking rock-et-rye
When the rye was open
    The State began to fling
Rockets at the stratosphere
    A present for the King

Sing a song of London
    Paris and Berlin
Washington and Moscow
    Where the Ids are in
When the I's were opened
    They saw ne'er a thing
But Phoenix in the Turtle
    The Turtle on the wing

Sing a song of Bethlehem
   Star of all the Idmen
Everybody's Jesus
   Now if never then
Sing Phoenix and the Turtle
   Defunctive in the sense
King Jesus eat by Turtle-dove
   In mutual flame, from hence

II

BIG, inside the tub,
Rubbed hey dub-a-dub,
Little did with rub
Dub the spinning tub
Big-Little, Great-
Small; Big then ate
Little and his plate,
Small a little Great;
Little big as Big
Apple round the pig,
Apple little and trig
Inside little Big:
All inside the sky
'S voluminous eye
Whose singular surpry
Laughed as belly-sky.
So the dubbed conceit
Played nursery of cheat
To clear the I of sleet;
Wiped Eye dripping conceit
And tipped by tubby fear
Slipped into the ear
All the I's old gear,
Semicircled a tear
With blind sound . . .

~ *126*

　　　　　　　But Mary
Mary quite contrary
Light as a green fairy
Dances, dances. Mary.

1950

The Maimed Man

Didactic Laurel, loose your reasoning leaf
    Into my trembling hand; assert your blade
    Against the Morning Star, enlightening Thief

Of that first Mother who returned the Maid.
    Beguiling myrtle, shake no more my ear
    With your green leaf: because I am afraid

Of him who says I have no need to fear,
    Return, Laurel! Dying sense has cast
    Shadow on shadow of a metal tear

Around my rim of being. Teach me to fast
    And pray, that I may know the motes that tease
    Skittering sunbeams are dead shells at last.

Then, timeless Muse, reverse my time; unfreeze
    All that I was in your congenial heat;
    Tune me in recollection to appease

The hour when, as I sauntered down our street,
    I saw a young man there, headless, whose hand
    Hung limp; it dangled at his hidden feet

I could not see how, in the fading band
    Of low light; nor did I feel alarm
    But felt, under my eyelids, grains of sand.

As, from their childhood, all men speak the charm
    And secret double of night in wakeful day,
    I thought that he could never do me harm

And gazed in stupor at the rusty play
    Of light where once had stood the human head.
    I thought what civil greeting I might say;

And could I leave the astonished oath unsaid
    That stuck to my palate in a gagging lump?
    Who could have told if he were live or dead?

Retreating sideways to a ragged clump
    Of buckberry bushes in the vacant lot,
    I looked more closely at the purple stump—

At the heart, three buttons down below the clot,
    Then down to where, the rigid shanks depending,
    Blue grass instead of feet grew in the slot.

'If you live here,' I said to the unbending
    Citizen, 'it will not seem to you
    Improper if I linger on, defending

Myself from what I hate but ought to do
    To put us in a fast ungreening grave
    Together, lest you turn out to be true

And I publicly lose face.' What could save
    One's manly honor with the football coach—
    My modest hybris, were I his known slave?

Our manners had no phrase to let me broach
    To friends the secret of a friend gone lame.
    How could I know this friend without reproach?

What a question! Whence the question came
    I am still questing in the poor boy's curse,
    Witching for water in a waste of shame.

Thence, flow! conceit and motion to rehearse
 Pastoral terrors of youth still in the man,
 Torsions of sleep, in emblematic verse

Rattling like dice unless the verse shall scan
 All chance away; and let me touch the hem
 Of him who spread his triptych like a fan.

Meanwhile the scarecrow, man all coat and stem,
 Neither dead nor living, never in this world—
 In what worlds, or in what has essenced them,

I did not know until one day I whirled
 Towards a suggesting presence in my room
 And saw in the waving mirror (glass swirled

By old blowers) a black trunk without bloom—
 Body that once had moved my face and feet.
 My secret was his father, I his tomb.

(By *I* I mean iambics willed and neat;
 I mean by *I* God's image made uncouth;
 By eye I mean the busy, lurked, discrete

Mandible world sharp as a broken tooth.)
 And then rose in the man a small half-hell
 Where love disordered, shade of pompous youth,

Clutched shades forbearing in a family well;
 Where the sleek senses of the simple child
 Came back to rack spirit that could not tell

Natural time: the eyes, recauled, enisled
 In the dreamt cave by shadowy womb of beam,
 Had played swimmer of night—the moist and mild!

Now take him, Virgin Muse, up the deeper stream:
    As a lost bee returning to the hive,
    Cell after honeyed cell of sounding dream—

Swimmer of noonday, lean for the perfect dive
    To the dead Mother's face, whose subtile down
    You had not seen take amber light alive.

1952

The Swimmers

SCENE: *Montgomery County,*
Kentucky, July 1911

Kentucky water, clear springs: a boy fleeing
    To water under the dry Kentucky sun,
    His four little friends in tandem with him, seeing

Long shadows of grapevine wriggle and run
    Over the green swirl; mullein under the ear
    Soft as Nausicaä's palm; sullen fun

Savage as childhood's thin harmonious tear:
    O fountain, bosom source undying-dead
    Replenish me the spring of love and fear

And give me back the eye that looked and fled
    When a thrush idling in the tulip tree
    Unwound the cold dream of the copperhead.

—Along the creek the road was winding; we
    Felt the quicksilver sky. I see again
    The shrill companions of that odyssey:

Bill Eaton, Charlie Watson, 'Nigger' Layne
    The doctor's son, Harry Duèsler who played
    The flute; and Tate, with water on the brain.

Dog-days: the dusty leaves where rain delayed
    Hung low on poison-oak and scuppernong,
    And we were following the active shade

Of water, that bells and bickers all night long.
    'No more'n a mile,' Layne said. All five stood still.
    Listening, I heard what seemed at first a song;

Peering, I heard the hooves come down the hill.
    The posse passed, twelve horse; the leader's face
    Was worn as limestone on an ancient sill.

Then, as sleepwalkers shift from a hard place
    In bed, and rising to keep a formal pledge
    Descend a ladder into empty space,

We scuttled down the bank below a ledge
    And marched stiff-legged in our common fright
    Along a hog-track by the riffle's edge:

Into a world where sound shaded the sight
    Dropped the dull hooves again; the horsemen came
    Again, all but the leader: it was night

Momently and I feared: eleven same
    Jesus-Christers unmembered and unmade,
    Whose Corpse had died again in dirty shame.

The bank then levelling in a speckled glade,
    We stopped to breathe above the swimming-hole;
    I gazed at its reticulated shade

Recoiling in blue fear, and felt it roll
    Over my ears and eyes and lift my hair
    Like seaweed tossing on a sunk atoll.

I rose again. Borne on the copper air
    A distant voice green as a funeral wreath
    Against a grave: 'That dead nigger there.'

The melancholy sheriff slouched beneath
    A giant sycamore; shaking his head
    He plucked a sassafras twig and picked his teeth:

'We come too late.' He spoke to the tired dead
    Whose ragged shirt soaked up the viscous flow
    Of blood in which It lay discomfited.

A butting horse-fly gave one ear a blow
    And glanced off, as the sheriff kicked the rope
    Loose from the neck and hooked it with his toe

Away from the blood.—I looked back down the slope:
    The friends were gone that I had hoped to greet.—
    A single horseman came at a slow lope

And pulled up at the hanged man's horny feet;
    The sheriff noosed the feet, the other end
    The stranger tied to his pommel in a neat

Slip-knot. I saw the Negro's body bend
    And straighten, as a fish-line cast transverse
    Yields to the current that it must subtend.

The sheriff's Goddamn was a murmured curse
    Not for the dead but for the blinding dust
    That boxed the cortège in a cloudy hearse

And dragged it towards our town. I knew I must
    Not stay till twilight in that silent road;
    Sliding my bare feet into the warm crust,

I hopped the stonecrop like a panting toad
    Mouth open, following the heaving cloud
    That floated to the court-house square its load

Of limber corpse that took the sun for shroud.
    There were three figures in the dying sun
    Whose light were company where three was crowd.

My breath crackled the dead air like a shotgun
    As, sheriff and the stranger disappearing,
    The faceless head lay still. I could not run

Or walk, but stood. Alone in the public clearing
    This private thing was owned by all the town,
    Though never claimed by us within my hearing.

1953

The Buried Lake

Ego mater pulchrae dilectionis, et timoris,
et agnitionis, et sanctae spei.

Lady of light, I would admit a dream
    To you, if you would take it in your hand.
    Will you not let it in a gentle stream

Of living blood? How else may I remand
    Your light if not as pulse upon your ear?
    Since I have dreamt this dream at your command,

If it shall bring my edge of darkness near
    I pray you do not let the edging slough
    To blind me, but light up my edge of fear.

The Way and the way back are long and rough
    Where Myrtle twines with Laurel—single glow
    Of leaf, your own imponderable stuff

Of light in which you set my time to flow
    In childhood, when I tried to catch each flake
    And hold it to deny the world of snow.

—The night was tepid. I had kept opaque
    Down deeper than the canyons undersea
    The sullen spectrum of a buried lake

Nobody saw; not seen even by me;
    And now I pray you mirror my mind, styled
    To spring its waters to my memory.

I fumbled all night long, an ageing child
    Fled like a squirrel to a hollow bole
    To play toy soldier, Tiny Tim, or the mild

Babes-in-the-Woods: sunk in their leafy hole,
    The terror of their sleep I could not tell
    Until your gracing light reduced the toll.

I stumbled all night long on sand and shell
    By a lakeshore where time, unfaced, was dark;
    I grazed with my left foot a pinched hotel

Where a sick dog coughed out a sickly cark
    To let me in. Inside I saw no man,
    But benches ranged the wall as round a park—

Sputtering gas-jet, ceiling without span,
    Where thinning air lay on my cheek like tin;
    But then exulting in my secret plan,

I laid my top hat to one side; my chin
    Was ready, I unsnapped the lyric case;
    I had come there to play my violin.

Erect and sinuous as Valence lace
    Old ladies wore, the bow began to fill
    The shining box—whence came a dreaming face,

Small dancing girl who gave the smell of dill
    In pelts of mordents on a minor third
    From my cadenza for the Devil's Trill.

No, no! her quick hand said in a soft surd.
    She locked the fiddle up and was not there.
    I mourned the death of youth without a word.

And could I go where air was not dead air?
    My friend Jack Locke, scholar and gentleman,
    Gazed down upon me with a friendly glare,

Flicking his nose as if about to scan
    My verse; he plucked from his moustache one hair
    Letting it fall like gravel in a pan,

And went as mist upon the browning air
    Away from the durable lake, the blind hotel,
    Leaving me guilted on a moving stair

Upwards, down which I regularly fell
    Tail backwards, till I caught the music room
    Empty, like a gaol without a cell.

'If I am now alone I may resume
    The grey sonata'—but the box was gone;
    Instead I heard three footfalls, a light broom

Dusting the silted air, which now put on
    (Like Pier Francesca sunning a shady wall)
    A stately woman who in sorrow shone.

I rose; she moved, she glided towards the hall;
    I took her hand but then would set her free.
    'My Love,' I said.—'I'm back to give you all,'

She said, 'my love.' (Under the dogwood tree
    In bloom, where I had held her first beneath
    The coiled black hair, she turned and smiled at me.)

I hid the blade within the melic sheath
    And tossed her head—but it was not her head:
    Another's searching skull whose drying teeth

Crumbled me all night long and I was dead.
   Down, down below the wave that turned me round,
   Head downwards where the Head of God had sped

On the third day; where nature had unwound
   And ravelled her green that she had softly laved—
   The green reviving spray now slowly drowned

Me, since the shuttling eye would not be saved.
   In the tart undersea of slipping night
   The dream whispered, while sight within me, caved,

Deprived, poured stinging dark on cold delight,
   And multitudinous whined invisible bees;
   All grace being lost, and its considering rite,

Till come to midmost May I bent my knees,
   Santa Lucia! at noon—the prudent shore,
   The lake flashing green fins through amber trees—

And knew I had not read your eye before
   You played it in the flowing scale of glance;
   I had not thought that I could read the score,

And yet how vexed, bitter, and hard the trance
   Of light—how I resented Lucy's play!
   Better stay dead, better not try the lance

In the living bowl: living we have one way
   For all time in the twin darks where light dies
   To live: forget that you too lost the day

Yet finding it refound it Lucy-guise
   As I, refinding where two shadows meet,
   Took from the burning umbrage mirroring eyes

Like Tellico blue upon a golden sheet
      Spread out for all our stupor. Lady coming,
      Lady not going, come Lady come: I greet

You in the double of our eyes—humming
      Miles of lightning where, in a pastoral scene,
      The fretting pipe is lucent and becoming.

I thought of ways to keep this image green
      (Until the leaf unfold the formal cherry)
      In an off season when the eye is lean

With an inward gaze upon the wild strawberry,
      Cape jasmine, wild azalea, eglantine—
      All the sad eclogue that will soon be merry:

And knew that nature could not more refine
      What it had given in a looking-glass
      And held there, after the living body's line

Has moved wherever it must move—wild grass
      Inching the earth; and the quicksilver art
      Throws back the invisible but lightning mass

To inhabit the room; for I have seen it part
      The palpable air, the air close up above
      And under you, light Lucy, light of heart—

Light choir upon my shoulder, speaking Dove
      The dream is over and the dark expired.
      I knew that I had known enduring love.

1953

Sonnet

Uxori meae quae aetatem bonam habet
Filioque nostro qui bimus est

Could I be sure that I shall see the day
When of the love in this young woman's eyes
And of the love of him whose youth decries
My age, I might a hundredth part repay;
Or would interior time, that could delay
The sentence chronic with the last assize,
Start running backwards with its timely lies,
I might have time to live the love I say:

Or almost time enough to con the glyph
That the mind's eye strikes on my shadowy wall—
Read it to learn how me God favored, if
I have the favor to know Him at all.
Who let me love you two? Have I been wrong
To love you well who cannot love me long?

1970

Farewell Rehearsed

I   TO MY SON BENJAMIN   *(Aged six)*

Come to me darling little Ben,
And let's play pinching-bug again.
I love you as my spirit's leaven
To teach me how it is in heaven,
Where all is love; stay by me, son,
That I may know that love is One.

II   TO MY SON JOHN   *(Aged eight)*

My darling boy whom I shall never know,
My son, I love you in my deepest fears,
I'll love you when my eyes, grown cold as snow,
Will freeze to hide their moment's joyous tears
When gazing on your happy little face
Which I'll take with me to the fount of grace.

III   TO MY WIFE HELEN

When I have reached the shady underground
With but sad hope of coming up again,
I shall implore your ghost to hover round
And guide me to a land of lucky men,
Even luckier than the land that I had left
Where love of you was all the air I breathed,
And once I'd left it I was love-bereft,
For with sad hope my empty spirit seethed.

1976

PART FOUR

Translations

The Vigil of Venus / Pervigilium Veneris

Few people today read the *Pervigilium Veneris*, and I doubt that it was ever widely read. Those of us who had some of the classical education which was still more or less compulsory in the colleges twenty-five years ago, did not read it in the Latin classes. Late Latin of the Decadence did not appear conspicuously in undergraduate 'courses', the purpose of which was to hold up models of 'purity' in the language and not to explore the range of the Latin sensibility in poetry. I came upon the poem, I think in 1917, in the usual way, in *Marius the Epicurean*, where Pater gives us a somewhat overdone reconstruction of the circumstances of its origin. I looked up the Latin text and was disappointed. I was still too close to Swinburne in my adolescent revolt against his influence to read properly any poem about pagan love; I read the *Pervigilium* with Swinburne's sensibility, and heard it in his language, having then at any rate neither sensibility nor language of my own; and I disliked it. I did not look at the poem again until 1930, when I tried to work out a translation of the famous refrain. My attempt at this failed.

I go into this personal history in order to say what is obvious, that most verse is written accidentally, translations not excepted. In the fall of 1942 the refrain of the *Pervigilium* came back to me and for several days kept running through my head; then I suddenly knew that I 'had' it. I had it, that is to say, in language that somewhat resembled English and in a metre that the English language can be written in: plain iambic pentametre, with anapaestic substitutions for the frequent falling rhythms of the original. The Latin is in trochaic septenarii, seven-footed lines with, at the end, an extra syllable which is usually accented, making eight accents; the metre, in fact, of Tennyson's *Locksley Hall*, which was actually used by some of the early translators of the *Pervigilium*. Except for certain special purposes it is an impossible metre in English, for unless the extra accented syllable at the end is managed with great skill the line will break down into units of four and three and sound like a Wesleyan hymn—a high price to pay for metrical fidelity to a foreign original.

The poem is supposed by some scholars to have been written as early as the reign of Hadrian (A.D. 117–138) by a man named Florus, who was better known as historian and rhetorician than as poet. This conjecture is based upon the scholars' feeling that the poem ought to have been written then, since under Hadrian the trinoctium of Venus, the spring ritual of the cult of Dione, or Venus Genetrix, whom the poem celebrates as the principle of sexual reproduction in nature, was officially encouraged and even given the dignity of a state religion. But certain features of the poem might place it much later, as late, perhaps, as the Fourth Century. The late J. W. Mackail saw in it 'a certain affinity of style and spirit' with the Eclogues of Nemesianus of Carthage (*circa* A.D. 285), and an even more striking resemblance to the fragments of Tiberianus, another African poet, who wrote around A.D. 350. If I were entitled to an opinion I should side with Mackail, for although the simplified syntax and the stressed verse could have been written as early as Hadrian, it is not probable that they were: the language of the poem seems to stand midway between classical Latin and late vulgar Latin which toward the end of the empire began to show, in the levelling off of the inflectional system, the influence of the popular and provincial tongues. The reader of the *Pervigilium*, who has only a little Latin, as I have, will observe the occasional rhyme, the line unit of expression (rare in the poetry of the Golden Age), the frequent coincidence of quantity and stress, and even in some instances stress crowding out the quantities of the vowels.

The delicacy of feeling and the subtlety of the simple language require little demonstration. There is, of course, a good deal of merely conventional stuff, for which there is no equivalent convention in English; for example, the standard references to Venus as the founder of Rome. This material, brought into our language, had to be considerably doctored in the eighteenth-century manner to make it palatable at all. I have not found any scholar or previous translator who does justice to the restrained humor of the lines about Cupid and the virgins. Up to the last two stanzas the poem is moving, it has its peculiar subtleties; but it is not brilliant. In those two last stanzas something like a first-rate lyrical imagination suddenly appears.

Observe how it works. The 'maid of Tereus' is the sort of classical parable that we have had throughout the poem; but here it is not a conventional allusion. The beautiful line:

iam loquaces ore rauco stagna cycni perstrepunt

particularizes the scene about to be presented as no other scene in the poem has been particularized: we feel immediately the presence of a dramatic observer, an ear that listens and an eye that sees. *Terei puella* is more than a classical allusion; she is a real bird singing in a real poplar tree, answering the dissonance of the swans as they strike the lake.

Is she Philomela or Procne, swallow or nightingale? Our anonymous poet is not explicit; yet in the next and last stanza he speaks of the swallow who has ceased to be silent and can now sing. We evidently have here the older Greek, not the later Latin, version of the story of the rape of Philomela, in which Procne becomes the nightingale, Philomela the swallow. (It is perhaps significant that the poet uses the Greek *chelidon* instead of the Latin *hirundo* for swallow.) Countless versions of the tale circulated in the ancient world. The brief summary by Apollodorus, who collected in the Second Century B.C. virtually all the known Greek myths in a long work that comes down to us as *The Library*, gives the story as it must have been most widely known among the Greeks:

. . . and having with his help brought the war to a successful close he (Pandion) gave Tereus his own daughter Procne in marriage. Tereus had by her a son Itys, and having fallen in love with Philomela (sister to Procne), he seduced her also saying that Procne was dead, for he concealed her in the country. Afterward he married Philomela and bedded with her and cut out her tongue. But by weaving characters in a robe she revealed thereby to Procne her own sorrows. And having sought out her sister, Procne killed her son Itys, boiled him, and served him up for supper to the unwitting Tereus, and fled with her sister. . . . When Tereus was aware of what had happened, he snatched up an axe and pursued them. And being overtaken at Daulia in Phocis, they prayed the gods to be turned into birds, and Procne became a nightingale and Philomela a swallow.

[Apollodorus, THE LIBRARY, III, xiv: Loeb Classical Library, pp. 99–100]

The late Sir J. G. Frazer, editor of the Loeb text of Apollodorus, says in a note on this passage: 'The later Roman mythographers somewhat absurdly inverted the transformation of the two sisters, making Procne the swallow and the tongueless Philomela the songstress nightingale.' While I was translating the *Pervigilium* I assumed that our poet had followed Ovid's version of the transformation, but upon looking up the story in the *Metamorphoses* (VI, 424–675) I found that I had not remembered Ovid accurately, for he does not tell us what kind of birds the sisters became; he merely says:

> *corpora Cecropidum pennis pendere putares:*
> *pendebant pennis.*

Yet it must be confessed that the 'internal evidence' in favour of the belief that the bird singing *subter umbram populi* is Philomela the swallow is not conclusive. If we translate *puella*, in the phrase *Terei puella*, in the rare sense of wife, the bird is Procne the nightingale; and we may only surmise that the poet, when he asks, *Quando fiam uti chelidon ut tacere desinam?* is hoping that he may become as the swallow companion to the nightingale. This interpretation has, I think, little to recommend it; but the reader may take his choice.

The symbolic power of the scene in stanza XXI is firmly grounded in the dramatic perception of the poet, whose personality has not previously appeared. It appears explicitly in stanza XXII, where this long, gentle meditation on the sources of all life comes to a climax in the poet's sudden consciousness of his own feeble powers. When shall I, he says, like Philomela the swallow, suffer violence and be moved to sing? It is this unexpected and dramatic ending that makes, for me, what were otherwise an interesting ritualistic chant, one of the finest of lyric poems. Perhaps in the Amyclae, the people of the town of that name in Latium who were called *tacitae*, and who, when menaced by an enemy, could not speak for help and were destroyed, we may see an image of all 'late' people. I like to think that the *Amyclae tacitae* were not Latians but lived in the Laconian town of that name, where Apollo was the tutelary deity under the surname Amyclaeus, and that having offended their god, the Laconian Amyclae were cursed with silence and died of their own emptiness of song. May we see something of this in the last stanza of the poem? If there is any external evidence for it I have not been able to find it. Yet is the poem not telling us that the loss of symbolic language may mean the extinction of our humanity?

The text that I have followed is Mackail's, which was first published in 1888 and which now appears in the Loeb Classical Library. Mackail's arrangement of the corrupt text into quatrains is perhaps a triumph of textual scholarship. The poem comes down to us in two badly confused manuscripts in the *Anthologia Latina*, a miscellany of short poems of the Silver Age. In order to bring together material that seemed to go together, and to improve the continuity, I have shifted in several instances Mackail's order of the stanzas, a liberty that seemed justified by the corruption of the surviving texts; for no one knows the original order. Where I have moved a stanza I have indicated in brackets, in the Latin text, the number of the stanza in Mackail's arrangement. For the translation of the first line of stanza XXI I am indebted to Caroline Gordon; and for constant criticism, to Robert Lowell.

A.T.

Monteagle, Tennessee
27 April 1943

Pervigilium Veneris

I

Cras amet qui nunquam amavit quique amavit cras amet:
ver novum, ver iam conorum, ver renatus orbis est;
vere concordant amores, vere nubunt alites,
et nemus comam resolvit de maritis imbribus.

> cras amet qui nunquam amavit quique amavit cras amet.

II (III)

cras erit cum primus aether copulavit nuptias:
tunc cruore de superno spumeo et ponti globo,
caerulas inter catervas, inter et bipedes equos,
fecit undantem Dionem de maritis imbribus.

> cras amet qui nunquam amavit quique amavit cras amet.

III (II)

cras amorum copulatrix inter umbras arborum
implicat casas virentes de flagello myrteo:
cras canoris feriatos ducit in silvis choros;
cras Dione iura dicit fulta sublimi throno.

> cras amet qui nunquam amavit quique amavit cras amet.

IV

ipsa gemmis purpurantem pingit annum floridis;
ipsa turgentes papillas de favoni spiritu
urget in nodos tepentes; ipsa roris lucidi,
noctis aura quem relinquit, spargit umentes aquas.

> cras amet qui nunquam amavit quique amavit cras amet.

The Vigil of Venus

I

Tomorrow let loveless, let lover tomorrow make love:
O spring, singing spring, spring of the world renew!
In spring lovers consent and the birds marry
When the grove receives in her hair the nuptial dew.

    Tomorrow may loveless, may lover tomorrow make love.

II

Tomorrow's the day when the prime Zeus made love:
Out of lightning foam shot deep in the heaving sea
(Witnessed by green crowds of finny horses)
Dione rising and falling, he made to be!

    Tomorrow may loveless, may lover tomorrow make love.

III

Tomorrow the Joiner of love in the gracious shade
Twines her green huts with boughs of myrtle claws,
Tomorrow leads her gangs to the singing woods:
Tomorrow Dione, on high, lays down the laws.

    Tomorrow may loveless, may lover tomorrow make love.

IV

She shines the tarnished year with glowing buds
That, wakening, head up to the western wind
In eager clusters. Goddess! You deign to scatter
Lucent night-drip of dew; for you are kind.

    Tomorrow may loveless, may lover tomorrow make love.

V

emicant lacrimae trementes de caduco pondere,
gutta praeceps orbe parvo sustinet casus suos:
umor ille quem serenis astra rorant noctibus
mane virgines papillas solvit umenti peplo.

    cras amet qui nunquam amavit quique amavit cras amet.

VI

en pudorem florulentae prodiderunt purpurae
et rosarum flamma nodis emicat tepentibus.
ipsa iussit diva vestem de papillis solvere,
ut recenti mane nudae virgines nubant rosae.

    cras amet qui nunquam amavit quique amavit cras amet.

VII

facta Cypridis de cruore deque Amoris osculo,
deque gemmis deque flammis deque solis purpuris,
cras ruborem qui latebat veste tectus ignea
uvido marita nodo non pudebit solvere.

    cras amet qui nunquam amavit quique amavit cras amet.

VIII

ipsa nymphas diva luco iussit ire myrteo:
it puer comes puellis; nec tamen credit potest
esse Amorem feriatum, si sagittas vexerit:
ite nymphae, posuit arma, feriatus est Amor.

    cras amet qui nunquam amavit quique amavit cras amet.

V

The heavy teardrops stretch, ready to fall,
Then falls each glistening bead to the earth beneath:
The moisture that the serene stars sent down
Loosens the virgin bud from the sliding sheath.

Tomorrow may loveless, may lover tomorrow make love.

VI

Look, the high crimsons have revealed their shame.
The burning rose turns in her secret bed,
The goddess has bidden the girdle to loose its folds
That the rose at dawn may give her maidenhead.

Tomorrow may loveless, may lover tomorrow make love.

VII

The blood of Venus enters her blood, Love's kiss
Has made the drowsy virgin modestly bold;
Tomorrow the bride is not ashamed to take
The burning taper from its hidden fold.

Tomorrow may loveless, may lover tomorrow make love.

VIII

The goddess herself has sent nymphs to the woods,
The Boy with girls to the myrtles; perhaps you think
That Love's not truly tame if he shows his arrows?
Go, girls! Unarmed, Love beckons. You must not shrink.

Tomorrow may loveless, may lover tomorrow make love.

IX

iussus est inermis ire, nudus ire iussus est,
neu quid arcu neu sagitta neu quid igne laederet
sed tamen cavete nymphae, quod Cupido pulcher est:
totus est inermis idem quando nudus est Amor.

cras amet qui nunquam amavit quique amavit cras amet.

x (xiv)

ruris hic erunt puellae vel puellae montium
quaeque silvas quaeque lucos quaeque fontes incolunt:
iussit omnes adsidere mater alitis dei,
iussit et nudo puellas nil Amori credere.

cras amet qui nunquam amavit quique amavit cras amet.

xi

ipsa vellet te rogare, si pudicam flecteret;
ipsa vellet ut venires, si deceret virginem:
iam tribus choros videres feriatos noctibus
congreges inter catervas ire per saltus tuos.

cras amet qui nunquam amavit quique amavit cras amet.

xii (x)

conpari Venus pudore mittit ad te virgines:
una res est quam rogamus, cede virgo Delia,
ut nemus sit incruentum de ferinis stragibus
et recentibus virentes ducat umbras floribus.

cras amet qui nunquam amavit quique amavit cras amet.

IX

Bidden unarmed to go and to go naked
Lest he destroy with bow, with dart, with brand—
Yet, girls, Cupid is pretty, and you must know
That Love unarmed can pierce with naked hand!

> Tomorrow may loveless, may lover tomorrow make love.

X

Here will be girls of the farm and girls of the mountain
And girls who live by forest, or grove, or spring.
The mother of the Flying Boy has smiled
And said: Now, girls, beware his naked sting!

> Tomorrow may loveless, may lover tomorrow make love.

XI

Gently she asks may she bend virginity?
Gently that you, a modest girl, may yield.
Now, should you come, for three nights you would see
Delirious bands in every grove and field.

> Tomorrow may loveless, may lover tomorrow make love.

XII

Venus herself has maidens as pure as you;
So, Delia, one thing only we ask: Go away!
That the wood shall not be bloody with slaughtered beasts
When Venus flicks the shadows with greening spray.

> Tomorrow may loveless, may lover tomorrow make love.

XIII (XII)

floreas inter coronas, myrteas inter casas,
nec Ceres nec Bacchus absunt nec poetarum deus.
de tenente tota nox est perviglanda canticis:
regnet in silvis Dione, tu recede Delia.

cras amet qui nunquam amavit quique amavit cras amet.

XIV (XIII)

iussit Hyblaeis tribunal stare diva floribus;
praeses ipsa iura dicet, adsidebunt Gratiae:
Hybla totos funde flores, quicquid annus adtulit;
Hybla florum sume vestem, quantus Ennae campus est.

cras amet qui nunquam amavit quique amavit cras amet.

XV

ut pater totum crearet veris annum nubibus
in sinum maritus imber fluxit almae coniugis,
unde fetus perque pontum perque caelum pergeret
perque terras mixtus omnes alere magno corpore.

cras amet qui nunquam amavit quique amavit cras amet.

XVI (XVII)

pervium sui tenorem seminali tramite
perque caelum perque terras perque pontum subditum
ipsa duxit, ipsa venis procreantem spiritum
inbuit, iussitque mundum nosse nascendi vias.

cras amet qui nunquam amavit quique amavit cras amet.

XIII

Among the garlands, among the myrtle bowers
Ceres and Bacchus, and the god of verse, delay.
Nightlong the watch must be kept with votive cry—
Dione's queen of the woods: Diana, make way!

Tomorrow may loveless, may lover tomorrow make love.

XIV

She places her court among the flowers of Hybla;
Presiding, she speaks her laws; the Graces are near.
Hybla, give all your blossoms, and bring, Hybla,
The brightest plain of Enna for the whole year.

Tomorrow may loveless, may lover tomorrow make love.

XV

With spring the father-sky remakes the world:
The male shower has flowed into the bride,
Earth's body; then shifted through sky and sea and land
To touch the quickening child in her deep side.

Tomorrow may loveless, may lover tomorrow make love.

XVI

Over sky and land and down under the sea
On the path of the seed the goddess brought to earth
And dropped into our veins created fire,
That men might know the mysteries of birth.

Tomorrow may loveless, may lover tomorrow make love.

XVII (XVI)

ipsa venas atque mentem permeanti spiritu
intus occultis gubernat procreatrix viribus.
ipsa Troianos nepotes in Latinos transtulit,
Romuleas ipsa fecit cum Sabinis nuptias.

cras amet qui nunquam amavit quique amavit cras amet.

XVIII

ipsa Laurentem puellam coniugem nato dedit,
moxque Marti de sacello dat pudicam virginem,
unde Ramnes et Quirites proque prole posterum
Romulum patrem crearet et nepotem Caesarem.

cras amet qui nunquam amavit quique amavit cras amet.

XIX

rura fecundat voluptas: rura Venerem sentiunt:
ipse Amor puer Dionae rure natus creditur:
hunc ager cum parturiret ipsa suscepit sinu,
ipsa florum delicatis educavit osculis.

cras amet qui nunquam amavit quique amavit cras amet.

XX

ecce iam super genestas explicant tauri latus,
quisque coetus continetur coniugali foedere:
subter umbras cum maritis ecce balantum gregem,
et canoras non tacere diva iussit alites.

cras amet qui nunquam amavit quique amavit cras amet.

XVII

Body and mind the inventive Creatress fills
With spirit blowing its invariable power:
The Sabine girls she gave to the sons of Rome
And sowed the seed exiled from the Trojan tower.

Tomorrow may loveless, may lover tomorrow make love.

XVIII

Lavinia of Laurentum she chose to bed
Her son Aeneas, and for the black Mars won
The virgin Silvia, to found the Roman line:
Sire Romulus, and Caesar her grandson.

Tomorrow may loveless, may lover tomorrow make love.

XIX

Venus knows country matters: country knows Venus:
For Love, Dione's boy, was born on the farm.
From the rich furrow she snatched him to her breast,
With tender flowers taught him peculiar charm.

Tomorrow may loveless, may lover tomorrow make love.

XX

See how the bullocks rub their flanks with broom!
See the ram pursue through the shade the bleating ewe,
For lovers' union is Venus in kind pursuit;
And she tells the birds to forget their winter woe.

Tomorrow may loveless, may lover tomorrow make love.

XXI

iam loquaces ore rauco stagna cycni perstrepunt:
adsonat Terei puella subter umbram populi,
ut potes motus amoris ore dici musicos,
at neges queri sororem de marito barbaro.

cras amet qui nunquam amavit quique amavit cras amet.

XXII

illa cantat, nos tacemus: quando ver venit meum?
quando fiam uti chelidon ut tacere desinam?
perdidi musam tacendo, nec me Apollo respicit:
sic Amyclas, cum tacerent, perdidit silentium.

cras amet qui nunquam amavit quique amavit cras amet.

XXI

Now the tall swans with hoarse cries thrash the lake:
The girl of Tereus pours from the poplar ring
Musical change—sad sister who bewails
Her act of darkness with the barbarous king!

> Tomorrow may loveless, may lover tomorrow make love.

XXII

She sings, we are silent. When will my spring come?
Shall I find my voice when I shall be as the swallow?
Silence destroyed the Amyclae: they were dumb.
Silent, I lost the muse. Return, Apollo!

> Tomorrow let loveless, let lover tomorrow make love.

1947

Farewell to Anactoria

Sappho

Never the tramp of foot or horse,
Nor lusty cries from ship at sea,
Shall I call loveliest on the dark earth—
    My heart moves lovingly.

I say that what one loves is best:
The midnight fastness of the heart.
Helen, you took the beauty of men
    With unpitying art!

White Paris from Idean hills
For you the Trojan towers razed—
Who swiftly ploughed the black seas
    Had on your white arm gazed!

Oh, how loving from afar
Led you to grief, for in your mind
The present was too light, as ever
    Among fair womankind. . . .

So, Anactoria, go you away
With what calm carelessness of sorrow!
Your gleaming footstep and your grace,
    When comes another morrow,

Much would I rather then behold
Than Lydian cars or infantry.
I ask the lot of blessedness,
    Belovèd, in memory.

1922

Adaptation of a Theme by Catullus

From the translation by Aubrey Beardsley

Carmen CI

Past towns, states, deserts, hills and rivers borne
By the first plane, brother, I've come today,
A spirit, to linger at your spiritless clay
That sleeps well-dressed beyond the reach of scorn:
Not glad, lifeless tycoon, nor sorry feel
For neither Bull nor Bear attends your way—
Ah, vanity of speech, what should I say?
The grave encloses you with technical zeal
For Chance, swift giver, may just as swiftly take.
Accept these costly wreaths for my own sake
(Death asks no entrance fee to let you in)
And for the decent sense of heaven and hell:
Take them, and think not much on mortal sin.
Now, brother, time being money, I say farewell.

1948

Correspondences

From the French of Charles Baudelaire

All nature is a temple where the alive
Pillars breathe often a tremor of mixed words;
Man wanders in a forest of accords
That peer familiarly from each ogive.

Like thinning echoes tumbling to sleep beyond
In a unity umbrageous and infinite,
Vast as the night stupendously moonlit,
All smells and colors and sounds correspond.

Odors blown sweet as infants' naked flesh,
Soft as oboes, green as a studded plain,
—Others, corrupt, rich and triumphant, thresh

Expansions to the infinite of pain:
Amber and myrrh, benzoin and musk condense
To transports of the spirit and the sense!

1925

A Carrion

From the French of Charles Baudelaire

Remember now, my Love, what piteous thing
    We saw on a summer's gracious day:
By the roadside a hideous carrion, quivering
    On a clean bed of pebbly clay,

Her legs flexed in the air like a courtesan,
    Burning and sweating venomously,
Calmly exposed its belly, ironic and wan,
    Clamorous with foul ecstasy.

The sun bore down upon this rottenness
    As if to roast it with gold fire,
And render back to nature her own largess
    A hundredfold of her desire.

Heaven observed the vaunting carcass there
    Blooming with the richness of a flower;
And that almighty stink which corpses wear
    Choked you with sleepy power!

The flies swarmed on the putrid vulva, then
    A black tumbling rout would seethe
Of maggots, thick like a torrent in a glen,
    Over those rags that lived and seemed to breathe.

They darted down and rose up like a wave
    Or buzzed impetuously as before;
One would have thought the corpse was held a slave
    To living by the life it bore!

This world had music, its own swift emotion
    Like water and the wind running,
Or corn that a winnower in rhythmic motion
    Fans with fiery cunning.

All forms receded, as in a dream were still,
    Where white visions vaguely start
From the sketch of a painter's long-neglected idyl
    Into a perfect art!

Behind the rocks a restless bitch looked on
    Regarding us with jealous eyes,
Waiting to tear from the livid skeleton
    Her loosed morsel quick with flies.

And even you will come to this foul shame,
    This ultimate infection,
Star of my eyes, my being's inner flame,
    My angel and my passion!

Yes: such shall you be, O queen of heavenly grace,
    Beyond the last sacrament,
When through your bones the flowers and sucking grass
    Weave their rank cerement.

Speak, then, my Beauty, to this dire putrescence,
    To the worm that shall kiss your proud estate,
That I have kept the divine form and the essence
    Of my festered loves inviolate!

1928

Sulpicia to Cerinthus

Tibullus, Lib. III, xviii

Ne tibi sim, mea lux, aeque iam fervida cura
    ac videor paucos ante fuisse dies,
si quicquam tota commisi stulta iuventa
    cuius me fatear paenituisse magis,
hesterna quam te solum quod nocte reliqui,
    ardorem cupiens dissimulare meum.

Let me no more, my love, be what I've seemed to you
    These last few days—a long, torturing fire,
If I in all my youth have done a stupid thing
    (Of which I should repent or sooner tire)
More shameful than, last night, to let you toss alone,
    When from your arms I kept my cold desire.

1953

PART FIVE

Early Poems

Red Stains

In a pyloned desert where the scorpion reigns
My love and I plucked poppies breathing tales
Of crimes now long asleep, whose once-red stains
Dyed stabbing men, at sea with bloody sails.
The golden sand drowsed. There a dog yelped loud;
And in his cry rattled a hollow note
Of deep uncanny knowledge of that crowd
That loved and bled in winy times remote.
The poppies fainted when the moon came wide;
The cur lay still. Our passionate review
Of red wise folly dreamed on . . . She by my side
Stared at the Moon; and then I knew he knew.
     And then he smiled at *her*; to him 'twas funny—
     Her calm steel eyes, her earth-old throat of honey!
     1919

Battle of Murfreesboro

    1862–1922

He shakes the dust from off his feet
And shambles down the dirty street—
The last man in the town, they said,
Who'd shot a hundred Yankees dead.

At every door he looks inside
Where pansies bloom and violets hide;
Some little boys offer him a cheer,
And only the town-dog seems to leer.

What does he seek with watery eyes?
A face or two, perhaps, or lies
That tell him Genevieve is there,
Behind the trellis, just as fair.

I cannot say he walks in vain,
Nor back of his leather-lips is pain—
Only no bottle yields its cork
And skyscrapers tower in far New York.

1922

Bizarre

Do you remember how last year we walked
Against the purple sun through pearly shade,
And stopped all breathless, lingered there and talked,
And heard swift pyrotechnics nature played?

Then, as the twilight dozed, we crept along
In grassy stillness; color flew away
And rollicked with our breath of leafy song
That skipped off, hiding, till the yellow day.

Do not forget! For those green times now laugh
In glee with sport and thought and lily dance;
And fate in vanity now leaps to chaff
Me smiling at her winking circumstance.

These thoughts are fancy-painted, and you see
Their tone is light because they could not be!

1922

Bored to Choresis

Inert and in the twilight . . . Peace is not hers.
The fireflies blink, there being no man,
To observe the ritual of her lips—
Autonomous and Polynesian.

With sighs more lunar than bronchial,
Howbeit eluding fallopian diagnosis,
She simpers into the tribal library and reads
That Keats died of tuberculosis . . .

Furthermore Keats knew no Greek
Yet was exalted somewhat on Shelley's windy tongue:
What absorbs the girl is the fact
That John, like other mortals, had a lung.

Well, it's time to dress for the dance!
More civilized than merely discursive Man,
Her rhythms are reptilian and religious,
Choreographic and Polynesian.

    1922

Cul-de-Sac

God took a crayon in his hand
And sketched a swift line of distress.
Who will remember how they loved?
Who will remember happiness?

The ringing canticles of hope,
The azure rhythms of his brain,
Threaded the years that else were blind
And lured her back to him again.

The largeness of mortality
Had met him sometimes in the dusk;
The stench of this day's prophecies
He perfumed with tomorrow's musk.

Then apparitions of the wolf
Outside the scrim came stealthily;
He turned his back; what did it matter?
"My mind has thought for only me."

His classic taint of otherness,
Changing his human blood to wine,
Smirked at the doorway of her soul,
Which he had told her was a shrine.

"Now here upon the laughing fire
I lay the gleanings of the years—
A mildewed faith, some mutterings—
And scorched from passion all the tears.

"The white arcana of the just
And precious secrets of her kissing
Are devils dancing on my lips—
All but the craziness is missing;

"So many words are they to me,
A balancing of pretty sounds—
Why does she stay looking at me
Like a scared dog with salted wounds?"

And hope was gone and demons lingered.
Yet was there ever hope in him?
I knew him when his teeth were sharp—
More sanguine was he but as slim.

And so the needle pricked her fingers;
She fidgeted but didn't go;
A faint forgetfulness of reasons
Kept her with him. Time is slow.

The ins she saw but not the outs;
The pots and pans conspired to rust—
It made some difference, I suppose:
Her stare was dry as blistered dust.

Who will remember happiness?
I can recall that they are dead.
I know that heaven cracked one day,
And only God knows what they said.

? 1922

Debt

A withered silence filled my chest of sorrow
With mildewed fancies till she came to me;
My world she made of laughter and tomorrow—
A lonely sail that gemmed a wasted sea.
Her wisdom was a spendthrift, lavishing
On me a costless cloak of fertile power;
She led me up a steep path to the spring
To taste eternity, bubbling in an hour.
But I forgot the equipage I wore,
The magic sifted whiteness of her mind

Coloring life; vaunted in burgeoned lore
Of riches taken, leaving a debt behind.
From her I got but gave no wealthiness:
Fleeced I the giver, yet am penniless.

? 1922

Edges

I've often wondered why she laughed
On thinking why I wondered so;
It seemed such waste that long white hands
Should touch my hands and let them go.

And once when we were parting there,
Unseen of anything but trees,
I touched her fingers, thoughtfully,
For more than simple niceties.

But for some futile things unsaid
I should say all is done for us;
Yet I have wondered how she smiled
Beholding what was cavernous.

? 1922

Elegy

Jefferson Davis: 1808–1889

No more the white refulgent streets,
Never the dry hollows of the mind
Shall he in fine courtesy walk
Again, for death is not unkind.

A civil war cast on his fame,
The four years' odium of strife
Unbodies his dust; love cannot warm
His tall corpuscles to this life.

What did we gain? What did we lose?
Be still; grief for the pious dead
Suspires from bosoms of kind souls
Lavender-wise, propped up in bed.

Our loss put six feet under ground
Is measured by the magnolia's root;
Our gain's the intellectual sound
Of death's feet round a weedy tomb.

In the back chambers of the State
(Just preterition for his crimes)
We curse him to our busy sky
Who's busy in a hell a hundred times

A day, though profitless his task,
Heedless what Belial may say—
He who wore out the perfect mask
Orestes fled in night and day.

    1922

Elegy for Eugenesis

Your death, dear Lady, was quite cold
For all the brave tears and ultimate spasm.
So civilized were your thin hands, I marvel
They too, like jellyfishes, came from protoplasm.

O ineffable cheeks of rhododendron bloom,
It cannot be you've withered so mortally!
Your husband is heartbroken—he said so,
Winking at his cocktail, talking dollars carefully.

Dead Lady, it is revealed that you were twenty-six
And died giving us an homunculus with bald head:
May your black hair darken even the dark Styx,
May your soul have no tears, forgetful of protoplasm.

We buried you in the unremissive ground.
I went home. Somewhere I heard the clang of a hearse.
You are very far away, dear Lady—
As I light this cigarette—and under an inscrutable curse.

1922

Euthanasia

No more the white refulgent streets,
Never the dry gutters of the mind,
Shall he in hellish boredom walk
Again, for death is not unkind.

The graceless madness of her lips,
Who was the powder-puff of life,
Cannot rouge those cheeks nor warm
His cold corpuscles back to strife.

What did he gain? What did he lose?
These questions for the pious dead
Are blown from bosoms of kind souls—
A scented sorrow, corseted!

1922

Fair Cuirass Shattered

One time I thought that sunset's flaming air
    Could forge in me the steel to batter through
    The hardy walls of men; that they, as you,
Would quake at onslaughts from a poet's lair.
We then lived roses; I had fooled despair
    And boxed him up and flogged his retinue,
    Made strong by cheeks and lips! I sucked in dew,
And dragged the world, a weakling, by the hair.

This hour is roseless; ruddiness is snuffed;
    Wan lilies, smutted in a dragon's breath,
      Are limp; and iron lizards track the earth
To crunch men's bones, and fledgy clouds are buffed.
    I suck in smoke! I smile at grimy mirth,
    And laugh to think that *you* had parried death.

    1922

The Flapper

All night long the darling daughter squirms
Wild where the Toddle and the Shimmy vie
In making passion virtuous and correct,
That nature may be told just one more lie.

Her mother is a lorgnette scanning all
The eligible men upon the floor:
She thinks of what their great-grand fathers did,
Eschewing her darling might become their whore.

A spade is not a spade, and it is just
That any tremulous twisting of her lips
Should be mere prettiness, or call it grace
The *canto amoroso* of her hips.

1922

Hitch Your Wagon to a Star

The dull conclave of crows'-footed faces
Twitches as the man with one dollar enters;
It moves a soilured delicate hand, as if
Displaying a marketable emotion on a string.

Hear the tom-toms, smell the warm rank beer,
See the curve of the synthetic waggle,
Let ancient visions impinge the modern retina,
Polish the image of a burnished Phrygia.

For I have heard that somewhere, on desolate
And traditionally inspiring shores,
Small ladies, possessing subtile bellies, knew heroes
Whose creed brooked no chaste asyndeton;

And somewhat later, in the cool of a fern wood,
One heard the grimly clatter of shields
Who threaded tapestries in the sheathing dark;
The courtyard rang with a feutering of spears. . . .

The emotion is marketable indeed
In spite of crows'-feet, which Strato doesn't mention:
Showing the contemporary irrelevancy of myth
And the understanding of a man with one dollar.

Make gracious attempts at sanctifying Jenny,
Supply cosmetics for the ordering of her frame,
Think of her as Leda, as a goddess,
Emptying a smile on Redkey, Indiana.

1922

Horatian Epode to the Duchess of Malfi

Duchess: Who am I?
Bosola: Thou art a box of worm-seed, at best but a salvatory of green mummy.

The stage is about to be swept of corpses.
You have no more chance than an infusorian
Lodged in a hollow molar of an eohippus.
Come, now, no prattle of remergence with the ὄντως ὄν

* * *

As (the form requires the myth)
A Greek girl stood once in the prytaneum
Of Carneades, hearing mouthings of Probability,
Then mindful of love dashed her brain on a megalith

So you, O nameless Duchess who die young,
Meet death somewhat lovingly
And I am filled with a pity of beholding skulls.
There was no pride like yours.

Now considerations of the void coming after
Not changed by the 'strict gesture' of your death
Split the straight line of pessimism
Into two infinities.

It is moot whether there be divinities
As I finish this play by Webster:
The street-cars are still running however
And the katharsis fades in the warm water of a yawn.

1922

Intellectual Detachment

This is the man who classified the bits
Of his friends' hells into a pigeonhole—
He hung each disparate anguish on the spits
Parboiled and roasted in his own withering soul.

God give him peace! He gave none other peace.
His conversation glided on the brain
Like a razor honing in promise of one's decease—
Smooth like cold steel, yet feeling without pain;

And as his art, disjected from his mind,
Was utterly a tool, so it possessed him;
A passionate devil, informed in humankind,
It turned on him—he's dead. Shall we detest him?

1922

John Milton

Your mind was wrought in cosmic solitude,
    Through which careered an undulous pageantry
    Of fiends and suns, darkness and boiling sea,
All held in ordered sway by beauty's mood.

Guest-champion lent by God, in might you stood
    Before the throngs of men; you helped to free
    Their souls; below, you played in heavenly key
Your heart's concerto—throbbing interlude.

But your suave Egoist, for selfish fame,
    Hurled to the bogs of Hell the Rebel Will
        And boxed him dark in freedom's smudgy hearse;
He paid blood-price for thought; his noble shame
    Was like the Greek's. Ironically, you thrill
        Me not with goodness, but with thundering verse.

    1922

Non Omnis Moriar

I ask you: Has the Singer sung
    The drear quintessence of the Song?
John Ford knew more than I of death,
    John Ford to death has passed along.

I ask you: Has the Singer said
    Wherefore his greatness is not dust?
Marlowe went muttering to death
    When he had done with song and lust.

And so I speak no other word,
    Nor ask where to go the jaunty throng,
For laughter frames the lips of death—
    Death frames the Singer and the Song.

    1922

Nuptials

To J. C. R.

She is a public deity;
And were't not very odd
She should dispose berself to be
A petty bousebold god.
                    Orinda

When noon-time comes the whistle blows.
Down the straight street in jagged rows
The multitudinous workmen shamble
Past Mike's saloon through swarming flies
To the weedy lot where they may gamble
With crooked dice and gorge stale pies.
It is the hour when stink and sweat
Subside to let the flesh forget
Affinity for brick and lathe,
The cold necessity to bathe—
And certain things one would forget.

The bones rattle, the nickels jingle,
Nuts and Sevens alternate,
A pair of shoes balance fate,
And Brady's tongue and finger tingle.
Let shoes be lost or shoes be won
This night shall be a night of fun:
Two dollars now prognosticate
An image supine and elate
For Jenny sweet will keep the date
Early or late.

The clock has struck a dismal clack.
They tread the same well-trodden track,
A hunger flashing in the eye
Which jutting bellies would belie.
A song is loosed, a fleck of jazz
I am the captain of my soul
I will climb a greasy pole
When six o'clock turns round again
And street lamps light the Dark Siren.

Along the muddy river's rocky brink
A troop of titans trudges in the dusk,
No stench rises of hyacinth and musk
Nor any pillars of the Athenians,
The dusk trails farther down the wharf
O darkness of impenetrable might!
The clink of empty dinner pails, the thud
Of feet, chatter of teeth, fetid eyes:
I have lived many years and many lies
But not before on the dull stroke of seven,
Have I heard whispers on the rickety stair
And rain upon the cracked window-pane,
Suddenly had visions of beautiful dead hair.
Eight nine ten eleven,
The arc of justice is the twist of truth
Achilles nine times dragged in the mud
Wearing my new amethystine ring
Mumbling phrases from the Book of Ruth
Down the straight street in luminous quest of truth
I go to hear the ladies laugh and sing.
Jenny opens the door and grins serenely,
Laughs like a sparrow, chirps, recedes, is queenly.

The whistle blows for five o'clock.
He rubs an eye, pulls on a sock,
Observes his bride still in bed,
Wonders: Now is she in bed dead?
She went to bed after I went to bed. . . .
The dawn sifts through the casement, foggy,
Lips are dank and eyes are soggy,
But leaps into his overall,
Puts on his hat, goes down the hall.

Buzzards float upon the sky
Shrilling a metaphysic cry,
Machines hum, midgets play,
Another corpse is hauled away
Hauled away

    1922

Parthenia

With pale green hopes and the gay colors flying
Of the rich shores that girded their dark land,
They burst into the temple where lay dying
An unknown virgin gutted by her own hand.

The shout went up like a half-strangled song,
Cutting the noonday languor into shreds;
The mob rushed out again and smote the gong,
Bearing the phallus over their febrile heads.

Still, at her feet, the thin-lipped lover prayed,
Beating his anguish on a tympanum,
As in and out among the few that stayed
Wandered the priest's voice from the adytum:

"Lay now the grape and the bright leaves of sorrow
Upon the altar beside her bloody hair;
Wash clean your hands and hearts, that no tomorrow
May find her unforgiven or unfair;

"The god has not yet answered to our pity
For the black vision and tangle in her brains,
Nor is there knowing soever in the city
Of the red histories that throbbed in her blue veins."

Then, as the twilight clutched a single star,
Cold wonder drove the mourners on their way:
All, for the riddle, swore to roam afar
Scourging the night and gathering the day.

　　1922

To a Prodigal Old Maid

Sing now no hymn nor chant a dirge
Nor weep for any dead thing,
Still in her veins an ardent sting
Her beating blood can urge.

To the white pale lily she is kind,
Rearing few flowers that are red,
Yet sometimes weeds grow there instead . . .
In the conservatory of her mind.

A quick caress she gives the rose,
Lilac, geranium—all in season . . .
Oh, if she might have seen a reason
For powdering her nose!

Too deft at lavender and chintz,
Too cold for wooing but not wan,
She dreams a springtime gentleman
To have come a springtime since.

1922

Sinbad

I sailed too long over that monstered ocean
Ever to grapple with the sinews of an emotion
Like this slave-girl's. If I could wipe the must
From the mildewed jars of devilry, and the rust
Off my lip, the taste of the red preserves
Of love would be as honied as one deserves
Who lusted with wormwood and with sickening myrrh,
Buried with a magic wife. May Allah keep her
And other wives from me. But this young slave—
For the Caliph? Well, only her thin mouth to save
My soul I can't forget, nor her slack eyes:
The oasis of age is sand and lies.
She's just a fancy. . . . Now the Roc was mad,
As I was saying; trickery, the one weapon I had,
Led me to a blind valley; I clung to its leg
And that undid me, nearly—yes, I beg
Pardon—I'll go on—unity I don't pretend.
Ah, give that beggar sequins without end! . . .
But the Roc. . . .

1922

Stranger

This is the village where the funeral
Stilted its dusty march over deep ruts
Up the hillside covered with queen's lace
To the patch of weeds known finally to all.

Of her virtues large tongues were loud
As I, a stranger, trudged the streets
Gay with huckstering: loud whispers from a few
Sly wags who squeezed a humor from the shroud.

For this was death.
I should never see these men again
And yet, like the swiftness of remembered evil—
An issue for conscience, say—
The cold heart of death was beating in my brain:
A new figuration of an old phenomenon.

This is the village where women walk the streets
Selling eggs, breasts ungathered, hands like rawhide;
Of their virtues the symbol can be washtubs
But when they die it is a time of singing,

And then the symbol changes with change of place.
Let the wags wag as the pall-bearers climb the hill.
Let a new slab look off into the sunset:
The night drops down with sullen grace.

1922

Suicide

I have felt darkness lead me by the hand
Over the hill to greet the singing dawn;
Have watched neat clouds garmenting heaven's land,
Flecking the sky like ladies on a lawn;
Bought pearls in the mart and rare white laces
Made by the harlot for the virgin's waist;
I have seen cities, deserts; kissed dim faces;
Dreamed in old temples; known the sea's harsh taste.
And from the depths of coffered memory
I give you these—passions of little men,
Knowing at last the untold part of me
Like an old song heard once and lost, and then
A wizened countenance, forgetting pain;
A light, a twisted thought, a shattered brain.

1922

These Deathy Leaves

Though the grey year scatter these deathy leaves,
    Black and blood-red, upon the withered grass,
And the frail swallow fly South and weary bees
    Hush their dull music, I think not all shall pass.

I think that in the swift white mind's brain
    Neurons flash images of a world
Undead and deathless, burgeoning again.
    I think that Spring will come this way, unfurled.

I shall not ask what answer will be given
    To proud questionings, raised when men are lonely
In cold house, nor shall I now be shriven:
    The Spring I seek is in a new face only.

A shrunken leaf settles: comes a face
With a quick sculpture of a fresh grace.

1922

True Believer

Young Abdul scorched in fire of a desert sun
And munched a locust crushed beneath his feet;
He thanked good Allah, and when the scorch was done,
He slept where starlight paced the sandy street.
All night he skimmed in dream down a dervish river
And heard green dragons sighing for his blood,
Till soon the beauty of it made him shiver,
And then he floated restless on the flood.
His ears pricked sharp; he cringed and cursed to see
A vague red Thing that shrieked across the plain
Like India's mad ocean . . . Agony!
What unguessed stab made Allah cry in pain?
Up wakened Abdul, belching wretched moans,
And drew his scimitar and hacked his bones.

1922

William Blake

Now William pulled the lever down,
And click-clack went the printing-press.
William was the only printer in town
Who had peeped while the angels undress.

'Damn this unmystical sweat,' quoth he,
(He was longing for the New Jerusalem);
'Now in sketching an evil spirit—let's see,
Should the skirt of Lot's wife have a wide hem?'

And William had dudgeon for the sightless beadle
Who worshipped a God like a grandmother on ice-skates,
For William saw two angels on the point of a needle
As nobody since except W. B. Yeats.

He browsed in bathetic books—Jacob Boehme
And Paracelsus—which never mattered;
But he mentions the Ohio River in a poem,
So Americans ought to feel flattered.

William Blake cursed the flesh for a clod,
Yet of some of his sayings we Moderns have heard tell:
'The nakedness of woman is the work of God',
Or that title—*The Marriage of Heaven and Hell*.

Now I don't believe William ever saw that ghost,
Or even the universe in a fleck of dust;
But maybe I'm blind, like a soul lost,
With a lot of psychoanalytic lust.

1922

Calidus Juventa?

Non ego boc ferrem, calidus juventa, Consule Planco.

We are afraid that we have not lived.
We are not afraid of dying.
Toss images to the indifferent morning
Amid laughter and crying—
Amid fitful buffetings of strangled hearts
While they are dying.

Draw tight the words of death shivering
On the strictured page—
The cup of Morgan Fay is shattered.
Life is a bitter sage,
And we are weary infants
In a palsied age.

1922

Long Fingers

The twilight is long fingers and black hair.
Long fingers are old paintings on the wall.
Long fingers stretch, with no equivocal
Blurred beauty, through the dark rigid air.
And I have seen long fingers that would stare
With fiery eyes, and then the eyes would crawl
Deftly across the counterpane and fall
Soundless, with a wink of mild despair.

And there have been long fingers like a stone,
Eternal, girded with an ancient ring
Engraved: *These fingers are not flesh and bone.*
Often I catch my breath when I'm alone.
What was I saying? An Egyptian king
Once touched long fingers, which are not anything.

1923

Lycambes Talks to John

(In Hell)

Why that wild poet came to me to damn me
I cannot fathom. On the blood-soaked isle
How learned he bitter songs of lost Iambe,
Or that a cup-shaped breast is nothing vile?

Enough of that. . . . I loved Neobule;
My love the Lesbian puritans despised,
For was I not her father? Yes, you see,
My dear John Keats, I'm psychoanalyzed!

Her eyes like poppies and her silken flanks
Like trembling leaflets kissed by wanton rain;
Her hair a twilight—*Him* have her? No thanks!
Archilochus should ne'er that thorax stain.

And so I parted them, and here in hell
We're drinking tea from a Grecian Urn long after—
Your Paphian Fanny let tubercles quell
Ethereal passion: I know it by your laughter!

1923

[A pedantic Note: Archilochus, the first of the Iambic poets of Greece, returning
home from the wars in Thasos became amorous of Neobule, daughter of Lycambes,
as churlish an old devil as ever lived. Because of some sort of complex or other he
separated them. After twenty-five centuries, the psychology of Sigmund Freud
affords an explanation.]

Mary McDonald

Mary McDonald, I met you in the street
    When you were tired and your head was ailin',
Yet you shot emerald perfume from your eyes,
    Hoarded from the forests of your ancient Balin.

Mary McDonald, you giggled as you passed—
    I wondered what the boy with hairy chest
Carved on the wall of his inexpensive spirit
    Memorial to your infinite unrest.

    1923

Perimeters

    I

In the cold morning the rested street stands up
To greet the clerk who saunters down the world.
In the smoke mist, in the five-pound coffee-cup,
Thin gorgeous ladies promenade, ungirled.
Hang out your heads, O small unthirsted crowd!
The band is passing, blaring to the mighty—
Down from the skyscraper flutters death's shroud
Draping the shoulder of a wrinkled Aphrodite. . . .
Well, Jenny, yes—you're right, now let's walk home.
Could these bells ringing now be wedding-bells?
When we get married I'll buy you a pearl side-comb—
It's a mean world, with shivers and racks and spells . . .
In the cold morning, while the unsure razor sings,
I have seen ledgers and lights and folded wings.

Come to me, Jenny, let's dance a bit tonight,
The long small tremor's at my back again;
Distend your fingers to the sleepy light,
Hide your pink knees from the gaze of other men.
You must be pure—go slow with that home-brew,
Yet sometimes, like tonight, you *will* be gay,
And then I can't, for the artistic cheeks of you,
Drown this unholy vision of your clay.
Wind up the vic, lift one heel from the floor,
Cushion one breast against a lonely heart,
For I, with prophetic deftness, closed the door.
There will be music jazzing as we start—
And after that, when wax eyes fix on waste,
There will be staring and drinks without taste.

1923

Procession

Faster, faster with no loss of ritual
Stiff minions without banners, a steady guard—
And have marched since fell the first shaken leaf
Into the withering hand of Ermengarde:
Crushing the silly meadow-sweet the hearse
Collects at every house the fragment curse.

The men on the hearse are deaf, every Spring
They hear neither cry nor sweet civility;
Theirs is the margin between breath and breath,
Life's last, death's first; nor fore and after see—
These must be wasting like shadows, are as brief
As the silken smile that stilled Correggio.

Gateways to morning on the dusty road
Open with jaws incuriously set;
Weeping we follow like the steady toad
Drunk with his reverence. The mountain cat
Wheezes the air upon each granite crest
Raised on the good life's burial in the West.

The laughter and the shouting of delight
Of children flexed into a summer noon,
Chatter of women striating the crisp dark,
The crinkled light of an imprisoned moon,
Stop and foregather, hesitate until
One rumor straight comes huddling on another
Of death, and death, and death!

1923

Quality of Mercy

You will not forswear the bargainings
I briefly risk at evening with your eyes
Lest, faithless of mercy for a little dust,
Some of your soul crack in its brittle lies.

We made a silence, for teacups, once
After cosmic gall had bittered a lidless night,
Then touched the dizzy apples of Acrasia, once,—
Once we were shattered with a storm of light.

Now let peace come out of the hard history
Theocritus might glimpse but never share;
Hold a merciful year, prophet of lips to spend:
Re-string the mirroring plangence of your hair

While I erect an unrevengeful shrine
Of the total business in an evening
(To your shrewd pity), lit by candelabra
Laving the grizzled plateaus of the mind . . .

This is no song of a restless purchaser
Of griefs, nor harmonics muted for a withered joy:
Style a tablet at every noon time, Lady,
With bold images of a timid boy!

1923

Reflections in an Old House

When death draws down the blinds in this old house
And drapes a cobweb through the ante-room,
He will laugh softly, while thunderous mice carouse
In these bare halls where shadows mutter gloom;
Then old men, passing, will consult the stars:
'Some casual beauty effaced his calendars.'

When an old time is over and a dawn
Of less inveterate faces meets the earth,
The young ones will stop a moment at the lawn
Of a withered house, before the incontinent birth
Of common flowers that nowise different seem—
That yearly shall take their sweet and golden dream.

Then one will say, 'He is not dead, maybe,
Who was mortality's unshaken lover
Who loved the spring upon the Tennessee,
The hushed fall and, again, the coming clover.'
None will recall, not knowing, the twisted roads
Where the mind wanders till the heart corrodes.

Shall more than this flout the slow botch of time—
Of how he loved high laughter and the lonely
Heart, and cursed a dissipated rime
Of weariness in a golden morning, only
To rouse a cold Helen where the dawn distils
Her bewildered beauty on feet-forgotten hills.

Death will bow down the staircase and go out,
Leaving perhaps an unenvisaged hint
Of a young man who, in a stormy drought,
Rebuilt these fields in a slender Septuagint,
Translating an uncollected interest
Of the sun buried in a winter's West.

1923

Resurgam

Life stood on the top stair a moment
Waved her last gray slander down the stair,
I will not forget her absent eyes
Her other smile like one rose
Falling, falling everywhere

As I waywardly hesitated
With upward fingers and turned lips out,
Dismissed, tossed to always a twilight
Amid stuttering houses, tilted faces
And I said, If roundabout
Into the stark portrait of a mood
I weave a bolder composition
Lines of forward conversation, pencilled brows,
Two of my streaks of vanished blood
For mouth and hair,

Why, then I said, Life like a found star
Burning here usually and there,
Will return and pose once more
Where she stopped once with stricken eyes
Bitterly, then closed an iron door.

1923

Tercets of the Triad

To Ridley Wills

this winter's revolt of the unbellied trees
one reason being they're all gnarled knees
like Mrs. Foerster-Dudley at Aunt Alice's teas

trees grope with itch for Spring
go on and itch Trees you don't know anything
about how Ridley went Younger Generating

Ridley you laugh with pulp red cheeks
Ridley you have waded with little girls in creeks
Ridley you were a little with unfevered brow for a few weeks
tactile unredargued! trees undazed with bitter
used-up biting blankness of sweat were fitter
come Fulvia no did the Pea's hairpinned tongue titter

1923

A modest attempt to render the Triple Triad of Proclus into an idiom understanded
of the people. It has seemed discreet to dedicate this poem to Mr. Wills, who is
perhaps the only cavortive survivor of the great Neo-Platonist's doctrine of Hupe-
roche (fertility).—A.T.

Vision Beatific

You may walk among fuchsias unloud.
Enter, attend however a drum crashing deliberately
Correctly walk with mouth unbowed
Rubato into ecstasy

Loop large petunias on stiff necks
Funucles maybe of magnolia trees,
Recoil on split suspicion, in silences,
Disjoined between Adonic concupiscency
And Nirvana of tweaking the
Nose of absurdity!

   Well that will I whispered suffice, turn round
   look at the violet finger (not touching it)
   of death dripping on you out of memory
   remembering an accident certain of Greece
   how your gods fell dead

   bringing brankursine strange with disease
   he came—so beware a finger violet of death

The intermission done and ices
come down
And I will show you tipping
The cold hardwood with silver toes
Maidens answering once jazz more bold . . .

Some have for wits and then to midnight passed
Felt sleep thud up the lawn on a crutch.
Over the sky spread the efficient label of dawn
Many dawns—spread this advertising Life
That must go say they till life is dead.
And I will whistle for you at the gate tomorrow
    dusk and you will come with washed odors
    in your hair, forgetting

What was dancing to you then?
We went from the high gate away
To a black hill the other side of men
Where one wild stag stared
At the going day.

    1923

Art

When you are come by ways emptied of light
You'll say good-bye, in that indifferent gloom,
To the quick draughts of old, yet with polite
Anguish of pride recall as an heirloom
A dawn when stars dropped gold about your head
And, so amazed, you knew not were you dead.

For, brother, know that this is art, and you
With a cold incautious sorrow stricken dumb,
Have your own vanishing slit of light let through,
Passionate as winter, where only a few may come:
Not idiots in the street find out the lees
In the last drink of dying Socrates.

    1924

A Pauper

. . . and the children's teeth shall be set on edge.

I see him old, trapped in a burly house
Cold in the angry spitting of a rain
Come down these sixty years.

                              Why vehemently
Astride the threshold do I wait, marking
The ice softly pendent on his broken temple?
Upon the silence I cast the mesh of rancor
By which the gentler convergences of the flesh
Scatter untokened, mercilessly estopped.

Why so illegal these tears?

The years' incertitude and
The dirty white fates trickling
Blackly down the necessary years
Define no attitude to the present winter,
No mood to the cold matter.

(I remember my mother, my mother,
A stiff wind halted outside,
In the hard ear my country
Was a far shore crying
With invisible seas.)

When tomorrow pleads the mortal decision
Sifting rankly out of time's sieve today,
No words differently will be uttered
Nor stuttered, like sheep astray.

A pauper in the swift denominating
Of a bald cliff with a proper name, having words
As strumpets only, I cannot beat off
Invincible modes of the sea, hearing:

Be a man my son by God.

                        He turned again
To the purring jet yellowing the murder story,
Deaf to the pathos circling in the air.

   1924

Credo in Intellectum Videntem

I can't revise these manners but I think
If the dissimulating jet, which is your eye,
And the restless pearl, which is your either breast,
Would slough their antic imagery and shrink
To impartial clay, like the dead fantasy
Of treetops, I could be shriven as the rest.

Good manners, Madam, are had these days not
For your asking, nor mine, nor what-we-used-to-be's.
The day is a loud grenade that bursts a smile
Of serious weeds in a comic lily plot;
Comic or not, heterogeneities
Divert this pillaged head with too much guile.

Breast, eye—pearl, jet: Madam, have pity,
Consider the virtuous poetry of my race,
How, strictly, even Vittoria piqued the Angel
By that much beauty he inserted in her face,
(Wherefore synthetic wrath may breathe a city
Upon any dim and doubtful perhaps hell).

My manner is the footnote to your immoral
Beauty, that leads me with a magic hair
Up the spun highway of a vanishing hill
To Words—pearl or jet, or coral.
Often however I hear the music where
Your sudden face old twilights vainly spill.

1924

Day

Chariot so strict chariot
Riding the cold stars to death
You are an 18th Century Lady

For, the easy sphincters
Of your eye quiver a while
Then are still.

1924

Dusk

Day hot in the terror of her head
Rots on a weak hill,
Span trees web the lank clouds
Slowly spill.

Fretted shadow on stumps
A vanishing husk
Of light . . . grey lumps
Of stone verge the hills with fears.
It is quickly dusk.

1924

Eager Youths to a Dead Girl

To T. D. D.

This girl borrowed no dim light of a star
    Nor ever night held her in a dark mesh,
A slim bloom she stood of the first larkspur,
    A wind of spring fluttered in her white flesh.

It was not only a surety of eyes,
    Of lips,—nor the crisp music in her feet . . .
A muted legend of summer-drunken skies
    Rumored from her, tremulously complete.

Wherefore we, who expend the thoughtless race
    Of youth for a little while nor seem to care,
Will take her Image to a secret place,
    Blind in a gentle tempest of gold hair.

    1924

For a Dead Citizen

He was the finest of our happy men;
He had all joys, he never thought of death;
He fiddled sometimes with his mind, and then
Shook off the tremor like a nervous wren—
Just once or twice I saw him catch his breath.

Or in the shimmering clatter of the streets,
Or shaking hands, or tying his cravat,
He was the quick intelligent fool one meets
Without an afterthought of charnel sheets:
He never looked at things as This or That.

I saw him once again. It was too late;
His pretty wife was sad; I didn't know
For I was out of town and it was fate
That the indifferent message of that date
Should be a death, the embarrassing dumb show.

There at the church they took him through the door,
His sweet wide mouth much as it was before,
And some said, bitterly bitterly wept his whore.

    1924

Light

Last night I fled until I came
To streets where leaking casements dripped
Stale lamplight from the corpse of flame;
A nervous window bled.

The moon swagged in the air.
Out of the mist a girl tossed
Spittle of song; a hoarse light
Spattered the fog with heavy hair.

Damp bells in a remote tower
Sharply released the throat of God,
I leaned to the erect night
Dead as stiff turf in winter sod.

Then with the careless energy
Of a dream, the forward curse
Of a cold particular eye
In the headlong hearse.

    1924

Lityerses

Twilight stifled the valley wearily
And from the hillside, spattered with fragments
Chipped from a broken sun, a cracked breath
Of dead and brittle song tossed its bones—
Ringing like dream-armor in a sleepy world:
As must have rung the harvest-song of Linos
Luring the benighted wayfarer to a death
Of bloody water in a heap of stones.

1924

Appendix

Ode aux Morts Confédérés

Traduit par Jacques et Raïssa Maritain

Rangée après rangée en stricte impunité
Les pierres tombales livrent les noms à l'élément,
Le vent siffle, le vent sans mémoire.
Dans les chéneaux fendus les feuilles évidées
S'amassent, sacrement fortuit de la nature
A l'éternité saisonnière de la mort;
Lors emportées par le violent scrutin
Du ciel, à leur élection dans le vaste souffle,
Murmurent la rumeur de la mortalité.

L'automne est désolation dans le quartier de terre
D'un millier d'acres où ces souvenirs germent
Des corps inépuisables qui ne sont pas morts
Mais nourrissent l'herbe rang après fertile rang.
Pense aux automnes qui sont venus et sont partis—
Ambitieux Novembre aux humeurs de l'année
Jaloux singulièrement de chaque dalle,
Qui ternit les Anges mal en point pourrissant
Sur les dalles, une aile ici ébréchée, là un bras:
La curiosité brute du regard fixe d'un ange
Te tourne en pierre, comme eux,
Transforme l'air agité,
Jusqu'à ce que descendu dans un monde plus lourd
Tu déplaces, aveuglément agité, ton espace sous-marin,
Soufflant, tournant comme le crabe aveugle.

First published in *Le Figaro Littéraire*, Paris, May 24, 1952.
English text of "Ode to the Confederate Dead" on pages 20–23.

Etourdies par le vent, le vent seulement
Les feuilles fuyantes plongent

Vous connaissez-vous qui attendiez près du mur—
La crépusculaire certitude de l'animal,
Ces restitutions ténébreuses du sang
Vous connaissez les implacables pins, la frise enfumée
Du ciel, l'appel soudain; vous connaissez la rage,
La flaque froide, laissée par le flot montant,
Des Parménide et des Zénon rendus muets.
Vous qui attendiez la résolution irritée
De ces désirs qui devaient être vôtres demain,
Vous connaissez le dernier répit sans importance de la mort
Et vous rendez louange à la vision
Vous rendez louange à la pompe arrogante
De ceux qui tombent
Rang sur rang, précipités au delà de la décision,
Ici près de la porte branlante, arrêtés par le mur.

Voyant, voyant seulement les feuilles
Fuyant, qui plongent et expirent

Tournez les yeux vers le passé démesuré,
Vers l'inscrutable infanterie qui fait surgir
Des démons de la terre—ils ne dureront pas.
Mur-de-Pierre, Mur-de-Pierre, et les champs noyés de
   chanvre,
Shiloh, Antietam, Malvern Hill, Bull Run.
Perdus dans cet orient des durs et obstinés
Vous maudirez le soleil couchant.

Maudissant seulement les feuilles pleurant
Comme un vieil homme dans la tempête.

Vous entendez la clameur, les folles ciguës désignent
De leurs doigts tremblants le silence qui
Vous étouffe, momies, avec le temps.

                              La chienne chasseresse
Edentée et mourante, dans une cave moisie
N'entend rien que le vent.

                        Maintenant que le sel de leur sang
Raidit les oubliettes plus salées de la mer,
Scelle la pureté maligne du flot,
Qu'est-ce que nous qui comptons les jours et courbons
La tête avec une commémoriale douleur
Dans les habits enrubannés d'une félicité sinistre,
Qu'est-ce que nous dirons des ossements immondes
Dont la verdoyante anonymité va croissant?
Des bras déchiquetés, des têtes et des yeux déchirés
Perdus dans ces acres d'herbes démentes?
Les grises maigres araignées viennent, vont et viennent;
Dans un emmêlement de saules obscurs,
Du chat-huant la singulière chanson
Invisible et tendue fait passer dans l'esprit
Le murmure furieux de leur chevalerie.

Nous dirons seulement les feuilles
Fuyantes qui plongent et expirent

Nous dirons seulement les feuilles murmurantes
Dans l'incertaine brume de la tombée du jour
Qui fuit sur une aile innombrable;
La nuit est le commencement et la fin
Et là au centre de l'égarement
Attend—muette spéculation—la malédiction patiente
Qui lapide les yeux, ou, comme le jaguar, bondit
Dans une mare de la jungle sur sa propre image, sa victime.

Que dirons-nous,—nous qui avons la connaissance
Portée jusqu'au coeur? Mènerons-nous l'acte
A la tombe? Avec plus d'espérance installerons-nous la tombe
Dans la maison? La tombe rapace?

                                        Laissez maintenant
La porte close et le mur pourrissant:
Le doux serpent, vert dans le buisson de mûres,
S'ébaudit avec sa langue à travers le silence,
Sentinelle de la tombe qui fait notre compte à tous!

Ode ai Caduti Confederati

Traduzione di Alfredo Rizzardi

Fila dopo fila con stretta impunità
Le pietre tombali cedono il nome all'elemento,
Il vento soffia senza memoria;
Nei trogoli spaccati le foglie appiattite
S'ammucchiano, sacramento fortuito della natura
All'eternità stagionale della morte;
Poi tratte dal violento esame
Del cielo alla elezione nel grande respiro,
Sussurrano la voce della mortalità.

L'autunno è desolazione nello spazio
Di mille acri dove germogliano i ricordi
Dai corpi inesauribili che non sono
Morti, ma fila dopo ricca fila nutrono l'erba.
Pensa agli autunni che sono venuti e andati! . . .
Novembre ambizioso con gli umori dell'anno,
Con particolare cura per ogni lapide,
Macchia gli angeli scomodi che vanno in rovina
Sulle lapidi, qui un'ala là un braccio scheggiato:
La curiosità elementare dello sguardo fisso di un angelo
Ti muta, come loro, in pietra,
Trasforma l'aria ansante
Finché tuffato in un mondo più pesante
Tu sposti in un cieco ansare il tuo spazio
Marino, e ti fai come il granchio cieco.

Reprinted by permission of the publisher from *Ode ai Caduti Confederati e Altre Poesie*, Mondadori Editore, Milano, 1970.

> Fuggendo si tuffano le foglie
> Stordite dal vento, solo il vento

Conoscete, voi che avete atteso presso il muro,
La certezza crepuscolare dell'animale,
Quelle restituzioni notturne del sangue
Conoscete . . . i pini implacabili, la coltre fumosa
Del cielo, la chiamata improvvisa: conoscete l'ira,
La pozza fredda lasciata dall'onda che sale,
Di Zenone e di Parmenide resi muti.
Voi che avete atteso la decisione rabbiosa
Di quei desideri che dovrebbero esser vostri domani,
Conoscete la pausa insignificante prima della morte
E lodate la visione
E lodate l'occasione arrogante
Di quelli che cadono
Fila su fila, spinti oltre la volontà,
Qui presso la porta vacillante, fermati dal muro.

> Vedendo, vedendo le foglie
> A volo, tuffarsi e spirare

Volgete gli occhi all'immoderato passato,
Verso l'inscrutabile fanteria che suscita
Demoni dalla terra . . . non dureranno.
Stonewall, Stonewall, e i campi sommersi di canapa,
Shiloh, Antietam, Malvern Hill, Bull Run.
Persi in quell'oriente dei duri a morire
Bestemmierete il sole che tramonta.

> Bestemmiando solo le foglie in pianto
> Come un vecchio nella tempesta

Udite le grida, i folli pini indicano
Con dita turbate il silenzio che
Ti soffoca, mummia, nel tempo.

                        La cagna
Da caccia, sdentata e morente, in una cantina ammuffita,
Non altro ode che il vento.

                    Ora che il sale del loro sangue
Indurisce l'oblio più salato del mare,
Sigilla la maligna purezza dell'onda,
Che cosa noi, che contiamo i nostri giorni e pieghiamo
La testa col dolore che commemora
Negli abiti ornati con i nastri di una felicità sinistra,
Che cosa diremo delle ossa, immonde,
Il cui anonimo verde va crescendo?
Delle braccia strappate, delle teste e degli occhi
Persi in questi acri di verde demente?
I ragni grigi, magri, vengono, vanno e vengono;
In un folto intrico di salici senza luce
Della civetta il canto singolare
Invisibile e teso semina nella mente
Il brusio furioso della cavalleria.

        Diremo soltanto le foglie
        In fuga, si tuffano e spirano

Noi diremo soltanto le foglie mormoranti
Nella bruma improbabile della sera
A volo s'un'ala multipla;
La sera è il principio e la fine
E lì fra le estremità della follia
Aspetta, muta speculazione, la maledizione paziente
Che impietra gli occhi, o come il giaguaro balza
Sulla propria immagine in una pozza di giungla, sua vittima.

Che diremo noi, che abbiamo la conoscenza
Portata sino al cuore? Condurremo l'azione
Alla tomba? Alzeremo, con speranza maggiore, la tomba
Dentro la casa? La tomba rapace?

Ora lasciate
La porta chiusa e il muro putrescente:
La serpe gentile, verde nel cespuglio di more,
Tripudia con la lingua nel silenzio:
Sentinella della tomba che ci numera, tutti!

Printed in the USA
CPSIA information can be obtained
at www.ICGtesting.com
LVHW091132150724
785511LV00001B/89